A DANCING FOX

FRANCIS PLEDGER HULME

A Dancing Fox

Collected Poems:
1949 - 1985

BIRCH BROOK PRESS

The poems "Dogwood Snow," "Death in the Afternoon," and "Singing Tree" first appeared in *Mountain Measure*, © 1975 by Francis Pledger Hulme, and are reprinted with the kind permission of Appalachian Consortium Press.

The poems "Sesame," "Jesus Rising," "To Build with Words," and "The Music of the Spirit" first appeared in *Come Up the Valley*, © 1949, Rutgers University Press. Copyright renewed in 1977 by Francis Pledger Hulme.

Birch Brook Press
PO Box 293
Otisville, NY 10963

Contents

A DANCING FOX

(after the print by Koson)

Children, we know this fox and why he dances
Ironic sarabands, tawny and white,
Balancing tail and toe, his black pads lifted
To hold in place that Oriental delight,
His hat, a convoluted flower of blue
(Melon or squash?) from under which he glances
Like any artist arrogantly gifted,
Counting the house, but concentrated, too,
Absorbed and sober, classical and slim,
However drunken with the dance in him.

Before a sly suggestion of bamboo
He foxly foots it on the lava floor.
He has no nose for what's over the hill,
No anguish with after, no fretting with before.
Art has no tense.
                    His reticent ears, the twist
Of his ambiguous mouth, the understatement
Of body's dedication to his will,
And yet of body's rapture no abatement,
No lessening of joy or moment's gist,
With muted heart and moated mind to dance
His lithe epiphanies of vulpine chance.

Fox is your proper existentialist.
In old Japan a temple guard; elsewhere
Vermin for gents to hunt and hounds to tear.

Children, all this is nothing so fantastic:
Fox thoughts are naturally periphrastic.

FOXGRAPES

THE SHEARWATERS

I have recalled, in the bleakest, stoniest places,
The bend of the sun, the mound and the flat of the ocean,
The silver gleam of a fish as the foraging birds
Dipped in their flight and rose in their hovering fashion.

Still in my mind I see them diving and flying,
Soaring over the waves after the freighter.
Daylight slanting to evening, I stood at the rail
And marveled at the tireless swoop of the sooty shearwaters.

Far from the surging ship and the shivering balance
Of bird, curled wave, and sense of time suspended,
I have solaced more than a bitter hour alone
By standing again at the rail and viewing the banded

Flooding of sunlight staining the sea and horizon,
Bonding the world with golden bars, and brighter
For the rushing-in of the wonder-promising dark
And the swerving, curving fall of the sooty shearwaters.

OCTOBER ORCHARD

We saw the orchard fruit, sun-ripe, forgotten,
Left on the highest bough by hurrying hands,
Hang for a time-enchanted spell,
Blunting the sluggish winds
Before the air released it and it fell,
Muffled among the musty, rotten,
Earlier-fallen apples under the trees.

Emperor-wasps and winter-minded bees
And yellow-jackets dragging their dangerous length
Rose from their pulpy feast with a golden sound,
A swirl of singing strength
Over the drowsing, drunken ground.
And following their economical rule,
Anonymous ants precise in minuscule
Printed the yellowing grass with thrifty ease.

Ourselves drowsy and drunken with love, we heard
A crystal wavering, sudden and sweet,
The minor triad of an unknown bird.
Hushing the question on your lips, I leaned
Across your body prodigal with love
To break a purple aster at your feet.
My fingers feathered the grass that screened
The fallen fruit. I lifted it above
Your parted mouth. Kissing my fingers and turning,
You tasted and gave me to taste.
                              The autumn's burning
Had warmed not the fruit. To our amorous mouths it was chill.
You trembled in my arms. Then we were still,
Hearing the bird again upon the darkening hill.

DOGWOOD SNOW

These oldest hills, that lay all winter long
Quiet beneath a patchwork quilt of snow
And balsam bough and blasted chestnut prong,
Laurel and rhododendron's darker glow,
Are waking now to all the urge of spring
And burning with a velvet violence
That smokes the thin blue air and makes it sting,
Flaming with life invisible but dense.

And yet, as if these summer-seeking hills
Remembered lessons from their ice-locked sleep,
They sift a dogwood snow that clouds and spills
And spreads in white pagodas soft and deep,
To lie between galax and fiddle fern:
Wisdom that seasons teach and mountains learn.

"THE GREAT ACHILLES,
WHOM WE KNEW"

Death is the silence that surrounds
The stiller chemistry:
Not loss but less that stuns and blinds
The beggar ear and eye.

Eternities of never shall
Obey the telephone,
The cobra spitting from the wall
In tender monotone.

After the stroke of words a weight
Of airless sibilance:
What greetings in the caves of night
When you were three days hence.

BRUTUS WOODS

To reach the woods they walked across a marsh,
Firm to the foot, but spongy underneath.
"Here, take my hand. The woods are there. Be careful."
Her laughter linked her words into a vine
That bound the man and trees and night: "No, no!
Look after yourself. I'm fine. I never fall."
He saw that as she laughed she swayed there too,
A darkling dancer on her island tuft,
Secure and supple, as evocative
And trance-like as the moon-enchanted willows.

The woods pronounced their ancient word to him,
Making an incantation that began
To weave the spell: the laughing, swaying woman,
The shadowed trees and clotted grass, the wind
Lifting the leaves and letting them fall and float
Under the mist like swimmers under the spray;
The sudden gleam far in the grey-green dark
Where moonlight touched a python sycamore;
The doubled creek so still he heard not water
But the diminuendo it made in turning
To bank its bed under the matted roots;
And, best, the music of the place they stood on:
As they had made their way across the marsh
Frog choruses had gone before their feet,
Ceased as they stepped, and then begun again,
Not shrill or loud, but intimate and clear,
Confident, as he had always heard them there
When he had come, always alone before,

To love his woods: Like walking over a page
Of music; always, as he approached the notes,
They silenced, sounding again as he went on,
So that he played the score by silences.

He lifted his head to watch the willows change:
Blundering goblins sprawling over the marsh,
Dancers tossing delicate shawls—no, clumps
Of tired old men absurdly hung in shawls
Who bent their weary, moon-splotched willow backs
And put their heads together solemnly.

He took her hand. "Here are my woods. Come in.
You like them, don't you? Say you like my trees."
She laid her hand upon his straining arm
And leaned against his shoulder. "Of course, my dear,
Of course I like your trees. I love this place.
You are, you know you are, a master-judge
Of beauty whether it's in the mortal flesh
Or in—or in a night like this. I love your woods.
But all this mist, those chirping frogs—I'm cold."
She laughed as if to soften what she said.
"You'll be my death, and yours, if I don't keep
A guard on your poetic crazy doings."

Her mouth shaped phrases, cadenced clever words
That made the smallest thing she said seem grand;
Assured he was, and pleased to hear, and yet
His need to have her see urged him to speech:
"You know I told you when we spoke of this

The place reminded me of Barrie's woods,
The magic forest set in the magic play?
Oh, let this be our wood of what we will!"
She parted her lips to speak, but then she lifted
Her thin white hands (the moonlight turned them silver),
Leaning against him as she touched his forehead.
Her fingertips were cool against his face,
And on her mouth there was a leafy coolness
As if she soothed what maddened him. He bent
And felt her yield, a willow hamadryad.
She had, he found, her gift of silence, too.
After a time he turned toward the trees.
The moon had passed beyond the curdled clouds.
He let her go and moved away, disturbed.
For now he saw no goblins, now no dancers,
No old men either, only twisted trees
Trailing their limbs along a leaf-clogged brook.
Oh, beautiful of course, but not—but not—
She came, before his fury found its words,
Trembled and whispered like a shaken tree:
"It's so cold here. Hadn't we better go?"
The moon silvered them both. "It is too cold.
Come, then, we'll go back to the car. No, wait—
I'll carry you. By now the path is soaked."
Blindly he walked across the silent marsh
(Where was the music the small frogs had made?)
But just before they reached the great machine
He faltered, staring into the woods once more.
"Good-bye, dear Brutus Woods." Against his ear
Her voice was low, and yet it filled the night.

Her eyes glittered like moonlit leaves.

                                    Beyond
Were broken clumps beside a muddy stream.
Quickly he turned the key, started the car,
And wrenched the wheel to take the outward road.

BE SILENT AND EXULT

Let crows in raucous caucus come
And foul the field of sacred grain.
Utter no sound of hate, be dumb,
Pronounce no syllable of pain.

Betray by neither joys nor fears
That you have heard and understood
When nightingales attest with tears
The magic within the silver wood.

Saddle the unicorn and go
To where upon the perilous hill
Mandragora and apples grow.
Eat of the fruit. Bear witness still.

Receive your gift of star or stone.
Achieve your torment, your delight:
Siderial in echelon
The nerveless enigmatic night.

MELON

Standing in the dark kitchen,
Tonight I ate the melon,
The one you said I might bring
Next time to the nursing home
Where swift white feet crossed the halls.

In the early morning I
Went to the market and bought
The green-globed fruit. But it was
Not quite ripe, and I waited
A day to bring it to you.

After the funeral I
Ate the melon in quick bites.
It was cold and delicious.
You would have enjoyed it, dear.

I will be there down the hill
Between granite and dogwood.

WITH A POSTHUMOUS GIFT
(to an old tune)

And if I die before I wake,
Come, good doctor, come and take
These old fond eyes, that they may brighten
Another's world, that they may lighten
A brother's stumble in the dark
When I am stumbleless and stark.
May he see better than I saw,
Beyond the letter of the law,
Beyond the Now, into the spirit,
Into the meaning, or as near it
As eyes can voyage without chilling.
Be witnesses, my eyes, be willing
To see the world, for all its madness,
Is yet a place of grace and gladness.

May in his skull my new-born glance
Repudiate my arrogance
And be a servant to belief
That has been slave to hate and grief.
When I am dust, oh learn, my eyes,
To radiate a bright disguise
As in my head you could not do.
Dark brother, may I see through you,
So long a coward, now more brave
In second sight beyond the grave.
I give my eyes into your care.
Now look on life. May it be fair.
Come, good doctor, come and take
This gift of eyes for Seeing's sake.

DAGUERREOTYPE FRAMED IN VELVET

1

A CUP OF COFFEE

She never let you kiss her in the morning,
Passing with a wave of the hand in the hall
On the way downstairs for her first cup of coffee,
Or at least not more than a brush of a half-turned cheek
Already powdered.

And she would not say more than good morning
Until she had stirred and tasted the bird-quick sips
Of her second cup.

But her eyes, over the rim of the apple-blossom Haviland,
Were bright with yesterday's words:

And we stood waiting.

2

CHICORY

A common little flower, really a weed,
Choking neglected fields,
A nuisance to keepers of roadsides.

But she wore it in her hair,
Looking like Mother Nature.

And later, in the candle light of dinner,
Floating in a clear bowl of water,
Its blue vibrations filled the darkness.

3

SILENT NIGHT

Stereotypes and sentimental lies:
When Christmas Eve was longer than all the year
We knelt—remember?—with candles in our eyes
Keeping our worried watch for fabled deer,
Creeping to bed and dragging out our prayers,
In fever lest the morning might not come:
Then morning, and we tumbled down the stairs
To the enchanted world of doll and drum.
Now drum and doll take on a sadder sense.
The plugged-in tree has lost its tinsel magic.
Still, Merry Christmas! What's the difference?
There is no point in trying to be tragic:
Put on a Ho-Ho mask to face the day.
We owe it to the little ones, we say.

4

TO THE CARETAKER

Do not cut the clover. Let the clover stand.

She would take the clover in her wrinkled hand
And smell it with delight:
                        "No, let our clover thrive.
It will hold its sweetness as honey in the hive.
Think of all the creatures its seasoning will feed
After it has flowered and gone again to seed.
Let it make its tangles wherever it will grow.
Think of all the little things nourished in the snow."

She would lift the clover to her fading eyes:
"After winter storms it will rest and rise.
It will make a banquet in fields of white and red."

Do not cut the clover. Let her clover spread.

LILAC LYRIC

At Richmond Hill in lilac time
A poet had to leave his rhyme
To find the answer that he sought
In every colored cluster caught
Over the earth in fragrant curves
That thrilled the supplicating nerves,
Promised delight, rebuked despair,
And consecrated seeking there.
His words dissolved into a mist
Of emerald and amethyst,
With darker purple, purer white
To celebrate the day and night.

Like music rising tone on tone,
The sun splashed gold on mud and stone,
And after sun the silver stain
Of rain more soft than dreams of rain
Spread on the heart-shaped leaves a trace
Of transubstantial shadow lace
Which turned to opals when the sun
Came out again. Oh, how could one,
However lost, however doomed,
Reject such joy when lilacs bloomed
And Time stood still—and Time stood still—
When lilacs bloomed at Richmond Hill!

CYCLE

Arms as smooth and hard as handlebars
Commanded the flashing circles to your steering.
A windbreakered lump of panic and triumph I hung
          over the front wheel,
A gasping obbligato to your humming exultation
And the wheels' humming.
As the wind expressed cool approval
And the gravel grunted endorsement,
Down the long hill faster and faster into the home driveway,
Leaning back against your chest as you braked,
I rode in serene highness,
Prince of the handlebar world.

Safe between your corduroy pistons,
I came into the family kingdom.

Then I went waveringly alone.
Then I balanced and guided.

"Once learned, never forgotten," you said,
"Like swimming, and dancing, and making love."

Now you ride forever, my brother,
In the endorsing, approving darkness of earth and wind.

ELEGY

Save your grief
For another.
Let her rest.
Every leaf
More than brother
She loved best.
In the night
Every tree
Was to her
Dark delight.
Every stir,
Every sound,
Dulcimer.
Let her be.
In the ground
Where she lies
Her great eyes
Slowly close.
Now she knows.

SESAME

Poor beggar, turn away from stone:
Here is a kingdom of your own.

Assert the secret of this flower:
How, in a lonely, troubled hour
A man may turn from desperation
And find a raptured revelation
Suspended lightly over the grass,
A loveliness where nothing was,
A slender stalk, a bell of color,
To dissipate the spirit's dolor.

Find the alembic in the leaf:
That distills the grave from grief;
That sets at peace the tortured will,
Crying in green, Be still, be still;
That speaks to the distracted body,
Endure awhile: it is not ready;
That answers the antarctic mind
Enigmas of its arid land;
And medicines, not coy or curt,
The mute entreaty of the heart.

Poor beggar, turn away from stone:
Here is a kingdom of your own.

FOXTAILS

BALLADE OF THE DEAD DOGS

"Er liebte jeden Hund, und wünschte von jedem Hund geliebt zu sien."— JEAN PAUL

On sleepless nights they come and go,
Those faithful friends of yesterday,
Whose only pleasure was to know
When I would walk and by what way.
Across the years gallant and gay
They race in joyous rivalry
And bark and turn, but cannot stay:
I loved them all, and they loved me.

Barney the swift, Bunty the slow,
Dennis, whose coat was shaggy gray,
Miss Tot, whose coat was golden-glow,
And Cricket, a little burnished bay;
Banda, Lady, and Duchess—they
Boasted a royal pedigree—
And Katy the Dane could pull a sleigh:
I loved them all, and they loved me.

And others throng. As shadows grow,
I make each vanished shape a ray
Against the dark, a shining show.
A dotard's sentimental play
For men to pity or mock who may,
It warms my heart again to see
The old true hearts that round me lay:
I loved them all, and they loved me.

ENVOY

Prince of the Pack, I have gone astray
And dealt with friends unworthily.
Grant me one boon: believe, I pray,
I loved them all, and they loved me.

35

MEETING

Careful—he is dangerous!
The reddish-brown diamonds
Curled at the edge of the path,
The triangular-shaped head,
The fangs in the upper jaw
As he challenged our walking—
All the warning a man needs.
But she, with glittering eyes
And pretty tongue extended
Between lapsarian lips,
Restrained my raised walking stick
And would have stepped close to him
If I had not held her back.
Oh, isn't he beautiful!
She cried, as the copperhead
Slithered into the stone wall.
Her face was flushed with pleasure.
We continued on our way,
And I slashed at the thick leaves.
She looked back at the wall. He
Was so lovely, swift and free!
From the warm tone of her voice
I had a chilled feeling she
Was speaking of an old friend.

RABBIT HUNT

Do not say this region never had its glacier.
There are frozen places in the heart, in the memory.
One had thought there were things under the ice
Buried from the precarious walking of waking.
The sudden thaw of their recollection is painful.

Your letter melts the tides of the past
With its stark news, the brutal details of the murder:
Violence has become now more than a thing one reads about,
And deplores, and is angry awhile, and turns the page:
Now a fierce hand at the throat, a knife at the back:
The mean, cold, dark street,
A thin rain freezing
(Detectives pieced out the puzzle)
The muted demand from the harsh alley—
Did they know he always carried his pistol?—
The furious refusal, the scuffle, the shot
That killed the old man,
Our kindly neighbor, so good to us in our childhood.

No one else is left, but we can remember
How loving he was to us in the tool shed,
How patient in showing the uses, and lending,
The trips to the mountains for hiking and fishing.

It hurts now to think of these things.
I thought they were frozen
Colder than the rough stones he died on.

Or the long-hidden fields he took us once to hunt in,
Broomsage matted with hoarfrost and snow,
Our breath smoking and our nostrils clotted,
And in spite of our warmest clothes and our eager stamping
Our scrotums wrinkled
Like corduroy pouches for marbles
We scratched with mittened fingers
And he teased us: they were cold
Because we didn't yet have any hair there.

In the ice of the buried horror, one warm recollection:
Remember how good the breakfast was at the mountain cabin?
The farmer's wife and daughters serving men and boys,
Laughing behind their hands to watch the speed of our eating
Sausage and hominy, applebutter and biscuits,
And the steaming coffee you and I, of course, did not have.
Like a faded snapshot in a long-misplaced album,
The scene appears as the thawing mind turns the pages.

Later just the three of us crossing the fields above the river,
Two small brothers and their surrogate father
Taking their holiday fun with a morning's hunting,—
"Come along, you boys are as good as a pair of beagles"—
Shouting and kicking tufts to scare out rabbits.
But it was too cold, they were well bedded
Or hidden in hedges beyond the old pasture.

Until at the crest of a field he suddenly whispers:
"Stand back of me now—don't move!"

Perhaps the rabbit is ill, perhaps it is frozen
With the cold of the morning or the deeper chill of terror,

But it does not bolt when he kicks aside its cover.
It crouches in the cup of its nest, its ears flattened,
Its eyes popping and shining in the frosty sunlight,
The wind whipping the brown fur and blowing the grasses.

I had thought never to see again, as I see now,
Despite the memory's reluctance to touch the flat, faded picture,
The silver flash of his firing
Or to hear the sound I cannot remember I heard then
As he shattered the skull of the crouching, shivering creature
That jerked at our feet and twisted and died.

Wildly we scratched our pockets and kicked at the broomsage
As he picked up the thing and shook it
And let it fall into his sack half open.

We never talked of that death,
Not even at night in bed together
When we would whisper over the marvels of the day.
When we were grown men, there were censored recollections,
But the shameful scene lay under the glacier of frozen innocence.

And now the searing explosion of your letter.

Now I still see myself staring in panic—
Just as I can see the grim street, though I have never been
        there—
Where the nest had been, the splotches of blood congealing,
The tiny heaping of turds no larger than B-B pellets,
And the curl of vapor rising from them,
Like steam from the coffee forbidden at breakfast.

Now two shots sound forever across the crackling ice.

ON THE HEATH

Blow,
Kind
Snow!
Blind!
Spill,
Rain!
Chill
Brain!
Flail,
Sleet!
Hail,
Beat!
Die,
Sky!

JESUS RISING

Now dogwood offers up
Morning's ivory praise,
Now newest crocus cup,
The golden bell that sways

On April's anthem wind,
The robin's fluted matin,
The tree where Judas sinned,
Recite in Nature's Latin.

For bird that chipped the shell
And flower that broke the ground
Know all the story well:
Now with a single sound,

Now with a praiseful voice,
This Resurrection day,
Bird, bloom—and I—rejoice:
Laudamus, Domine!

BIRDING: OLD SCHARTLE FARM

I

With one exception it was
A morning more notable
For literary echoes
Than for birds observed.
                    Wordsworth
Came naturally to mind
When after walking through woods
Of beeches and hickories,
Gums and autumnal poplars
To shame Louis Tiffany
Without seeing or hearing
(Unless down-in-the-valley
Unseen and overheard crows
Count) a bird, I came upon
A flock of juncos in a
Cleared space with picnic tables,
Fireplaces and trash barrels.

Lacking his computer eye,
I could not say ten thousand
Saw I at a glance of those
Clean, clever, adjustable
Birds whose slatey matiness
And competence under foot
Have won them tourist favor.
But give or take a thousand,
The number was noteworthy
(Good birders take careful notes)—

Certainly there were far more
Than forty feeding as one—
Oh, hundreds and hundreds more.

They were in migration, which
With them is vertical, not
Horizontal. They move up
Or down the mountain as food
And weather exert their force:
Type of the wise—here comes good
William again—true to the
Kindred points, et cetera.
(Though he was hymning larks. Still,
Lose a lark, gain a junco,
If Browning may join our stroll.)

They flashed their gray-white signals
Through the bushes, on the rocks,
And near me in confidence,
Chipping the air with their calls,
Intent on their own affairs,
For which they have found in men
Helpful if clumsy allies.

I walked back to the parked car
Feeling like a cross between
Edwin Way Teale and Bartlett.

II

A sound, a sight, hurled me against a rock.
Great God, Good God, Lord God, Cock of the Woods!
Irreverence and blasphemy? Oh, no.
People in older days flung words like these
Into primeval forests when they heard
His rasping drumming and stupendous squawk,
Or saw his unbelievable bright crest
Of poppy red, his yellow, white, slate, black
Magnificence. Or felt, as now, his eye
Glaring in gaudy rage intruderwards—
Woody Woodpecker forty feet aloft,
Flinging down rotten poplar bark in chunks.
This bird, as Alexander Wilson knew,
Excited "vulgar prejudice" in them.
We are more civilized. We take away
His woods and put him on the list of those
Endangered creatures we unite to save.

This one I saw was the granddaddy bird
Of pileated woodpeckers. His crest,
His cry, the royal way he let me stand
Beneath his tree paying him tribute
Marked him as special in anybody's day,
In anybody's year of seeing birds.

Undaunted optimist (read "amateur"),
For half a heartbeat staring up at him
I had the birder's wild recurring hope
That I had come upon the Holy Grail
Of those who haunt the hidden place for birds,

The Ivorybill—and why should not the vision
Be mine? I pay my taxes, send my dues
In to the Audubon Society
And am entitled to my avian dreams!
But common sense and a quick second glance
(Both good for Grail trailers) made me cry out:
O *Dryocopus Pileatus*, hail!
Words not too often heard in Buncombe woods,
Agreed? And Woody on his poplar perch
Must have thought so, or had enough to eat,
For at my cry he gave a louder cry,
His accent certainly no worse than mine
And far more suitable to where we were,
Flounced his gay wings, and floated off. He was
So much the monarch of his dim-treed world
Pearson's bleak speculation echoed harsh:
"It is quite possible it will not long
Survive the passing of primeval forests,"
Lacking the faculty of adaptation
To ways imposed by civilized advance. . . .
Unhappy words, if true, to think about
As I came down Town Mountain Road, adjusting
My rear-view mirror, running my windows up,
And getting up my nerve to turn into
Beaucatcher Tunnel with its poisoned air
And on into the daymare snarl of traffic.

WINTER SONG
(after Halldor Laxness)

The wind moans over the moor
And lashes the croft with a sound like surf.
Grimur the troll wants in at the door.
Thin snow falls on the thick roof-turf.

    My old ewe is heavy with lamb.

The only sound but the wind is the groan,
Enough to set your brain on edge,
Of Gunver the hag who howls for her stone
And frightens the squatting birds in the sedge.

    My old ewe is heavy with lamb.

There is a time for taking a maid,
There is a time for nursing a fire:
"Running blood reddens the blade,"
But the cries in the darkness cool desire.

    My old ewe is heavy with lamb.

There is peat for the fire and fish for the table,
And nothing to do but drowse until spring.
When the sheep is his own, a shepherd is able
To wait for the shearing and even to sing.

    My old ewe is heavy with lamb.

DEATH IN THE AFTERNOON

The old fox is finally run to earth,
Who for dim, musky years retraced his tracks,
Baffled the hounds and had his nightly will
In chicken yard and turkey pen, slipping
Before the screaming feist through the dark woods
Until he vanished into the morning mist.
Now breath is enemy to lungs and heart.
His bloody gasping fills the shallow cave
They drove him to and where he finds escape
Blocked by the rock and mud piled at the rear.
The hounds and hunters circle him and yell.
The feist cannot reach him under the bank,
But lifts his leg and fouls the snarling face.
The farmer says, By God, we've got him now.
He's eaten his last hen at our expense.
Stand at the sides—he can't get out the back.
His sons, big raw red bulls of men, bring picks
And shovels, batter the muddy bank, and call
And whistle to whining hounds and frantic feist
Whose little feet fling gravel like a stream.
His coat stinking with burrs and beggars-lice,
His tail a rope that beats his legs, the fox—
Merciless eyes glare at merciless eyes—
Shatters his teeth against the shovel. The hounds
Spring in and savage him, tear out his throat,
And toss him like a sack into the ditch.
The farmer slices off his tail, the sons
Gather the tools and collar the hounds. The feist,
Shrieking, escapes their hands and shakes the fur.
Thin rain begins to sift through the dark woods.

FOXGLOVES

RICHMOND HILL SONNETS

Darling, if you were not already dead
You'd die to know I've put you in a book.
I see you now, tossing your pretty head,
Giving me what we called your country look.
"People like us don't get their names in print
Except for notices when they are married.
Gentlemen, of course, must do their public stint,
But ladies only then and when they're buried."
I teased you for your modesty and manners
In such an age as ours, whose coin is brass,
Where private lives are loud on public banners,
And reputations glitter and shatter like glass:
All the more wonder, then, for your high passion
Braving the world in Cleopatra fashion.

Your loving friends, and mine, were eloquent
With counsel and decorum for our good.
They gave their grave and cautious argument
With candor we received and understood.
They talked at length of certain grief in store,
The price exacted by outraged convention,
Closed doors, disparities, neglect, and more,
Painful details it anguished them to mention.
What they advanced was sensible and vain,
Substance we had admitted from the start.
Their compasses were needled to the brain:
They could not map the mountains of the heart.
We heard their arguments and their alarms,
Agreed, and fell into each other's arms.

Behind us Washington was blurred and black.
Our headlights cut the sleet like diamond drills.
With two swift strides we broke Virginia's back
And hurled ourselves on Carolina hills.
All night we compromised with dinosaurs
Which yelled downhill enunciating death
And grunted up with prehistoric roars,
Their eyes as fiery as a dragon's breath.
Inside the car, relaxed and lover-warm,
Untroubled by the outward violence,
Nor yet aware of any other storm
Which might prevail against our love and sense,
I stopped upon a dawning ridge, until,
Pointing, you whispered, "There is Richmond Hill."

You led me by the hand through rooms and halls,
Showing the treasures of your noble home,
Where glowing richly from tables, floors, and walls
Were Paris, Teheran, Athens, and Rome,
The proud collection of a gentler day
Watched from their frames by those who loved these things
And with them sought to hold a world at bay
That pressed relentlessly: cases of rings,
Silver, and china, the bloom of cherished wood,
Old books opening still at well-loved pages,
Ordered profusion that showed they understood
Who gathered here the heritage of ages:
Yet still the noblest portion of all your treasure,
For me, your passion given without measure.

I bought with pride and brought with greater pride
To win the glow of pleasure on your face
A golden chain where cleverly inside
A watch performed within its jewelled space.
I laughed to see you laugh with such delight
And hold the costly trinket in your hand,
Turning to let the sun play on the bright
Reflection guarded by the seamless band.
The sudden gong of the grandfather clock
Striking the hour, and echoed from the shelf
By smaller, swifter tollers, fell like a shock
Upon my guilty ears. I saw myself
Cruel to chill our time with such a charm,
Love's shining enemy upon your arm.

That summer was long golden idleness.
There was no work and very little money.
But doing nothing caused us no distress:
We lived on love and aspirin and honey,
Spoke French to help me with my coming studies,
Wandered your fields and woods, collected flowers,
Made raptured exploration of our bodies,
And knew the time was magical and ours.
Sometimes at night we lay upon the grass
And heard the shrilling katydids proclaim
That summer and our happiness would pass.
We only laughed and spoke each other's name.
Well, they did pass: our loving fell apart,
Yet still that golden summer warms the heart.

The cat Bagheera and the bitch Mah Jong
Kept house with us. He was black velvet, eyed
With emeralds, steel-clawed, narrow, and long,
A Kipling cat of solitary pride.
Her mother was a spitz, her sire a chow.
She had the sad expression of a sheep
Afraid of thunder. You loved her anyhow
And brushed her coat, red plush easy to keep.
Bagheera roamed for love. Often at dark
We heard him singing under distant trees.
When he came home, Mah Jong would bounce and bark,
Then whirl about as if afraid of fleas.
She watched him drinking from his silver dish
And passed him in the kitchen with a swish.

How could we, in these cold, mechanic days,
When man's morality is wired to stars;
When mind, computerized to serve, obeys
Impulses flashed by governing quasars;
When eyes and heart are eyed by one blind Eye,
Utterance noted and recorded There,
Answer required to bureaucratic Why
In numbered triplicate—how could we dare
Walk out like children in the world's first hour,
Ignorant, innocent, dancing before a light
That taught us love was holy through its power,
Like children sleeping on the world's first night,
Beneath a floating lovers' moon, where yet
No programed foot of astronaut was set?

How did we spend our time, aside from that?
We listened to Kreisler, Crosby, Piaf, Ponselle.
We climbed a hill, followed by dog and cat,
To watch the river where it flashed and fell
Upon its rocky way to Tennessee.
We read aloud, we played at household chores,
(Napkins and needlepoint for her, while he
With ax and saw was busy out of doors.)
Rarely we drove to town to visit friends
Who ever more rarely called. We were content
For understated days to reach their ends
And did not question how or why they went.
It was enough to have our loving teach
Diurnal lessons, different for each.

Oh, most of all I loved you for your voice,
Reading to me before a winter fire
Pages I named when given my evening choice,
Plato, who charted first the heart's desire:
"The fair mind in the fair body will be
Fairest and loveliest of all fair sights
To him who has the seeing eye." To me
Timaeus' words spelled more arcane delights.
To him who truly has the listening ear
The lover's voice will sound the purest tone,
Beyond the power of other beauty, clear
And true, but understood by love alone.
I treasure all your memory, but most
Your voice that sings in me, a golden ghost.

Let us be cool and recognize this thing;
Let us be calm and handle it with care:
Love is a morning song, a petalled spring,
A flight of birds, a point of light in air.
No man of wisdom ever thought to hold
For longer than the taking of a breath
This April treasure in the hand, this gold
And scarlet thing that has an autumn death.
Forewarned against the wearing of the hour
And shrewd enough to guess its trifling gains,
Would not a prudent man take to his tower
And barricade the door with cunning chains
And never scan with hope the winter skies?
But when, but when are lovers ever wise?

When I am old I shall give up this fire
And take me to some corner and sit down
Where nothing will remind me of desire,
A place for pause, a quiet place and brown.
Even my heart will be a thing asleep,
The ashes of a flame that danced and died;
There I shall watch the slumbrous shadows creep
And hold my counsel with my secret pride.
Ah, this may be when I am tired and old:
Peace then will be a sweet and welcome thing;
But in me now the urgent blood is bold,
The only season that I know is Spring:
Wherefore I pleasure in this ardent hour;
Wherefore the flame burns bright, and knows its power.

Or so I wrote in my young ignorance
And so I read to you before our fire.
Your hand before your face shielded your glance.
Your voice was low: "Peace then, and no desire?
My dear, how little you really know of passion
For all your metaphors! You must forgive
Me if I tease you in a lover's fashion.
Surely that flame will triumph while you live."
Ah, now the loving years and you have died,
Leaving me old and cold, but where is peace?
Where is the quiet place? My secret pride?
The lusts I lash me with bring no release.
I thrust my hands into the fire and yearn
In vain to feel once more the passion burn.

We lay beneath the Bee Tree copper beech,
Its shining magnanimities of shade,
Its royal amplitude of leafy reach
Extending blessings on the love we made.
Deep in its murmurous heart the throbbing hive
Protected its collected golden sweetness.
We heard and watched the bees depart, arrive,
And never flinched before their stinging fleetness.
All afternoon we loved and drowsed and dreamed,
Rousing ourselves only to speak of love.
Your mouth tasted of honey. The sunlight gleamed
And made a glory. But suddenly above
Our heads a leaf released and drifted down,
Shining no more, but torn and dry and brown.

Peonies at the sun-baked garden edge
Glowed in their fluffy globes of crêpe de chine
Against the shadow of the hemlock hedge,
So that the curved hand cringed. Above the green
Enameled leaves the pink, the red, the white
Lacrimae Christi with blood at their center
Burned with an eye-assailing, pulsing light
As if to threaten hands that dared to enter.
Yet when I brought them to the darkened pool
Where you were waiting with averted eyes,
The pale globes of your fragrant breasts, the full
Lacrimae Christi wonder of your thighs,
They did not burn: they were cool to my lips
And to seeking, solacing fingertips.

A criminal of love, another time
I have been juried, judged, and jailed by her
Who was once more the cause of my hot crime
And signed the writ that made me prisoner.
Recidivist who, happily handcuffed,
Stand at the bar of self-recrimination
And laugh to hear my evidence rebuffed,
I have no wish for rehabilitation.
Pardoning boards need not assess my case:
Only my warden, with her double key,
Can lock me out and certify the space
That bars me from the bars of being free.
Since law forbids the rope, or gas, or knife,
Sentence me, Love, to servitude for life.

Mapping in blood its blind geography,
This flood that drowns its caves and swells with power
And spreads too far for straining eye to see
And surges higher hour by throbbing hour,
Began from rock-deep springs, fingers of flowing
That sponged the fevers of covers and dusty ridges
Until, its gradual movement ever growing,
It lipped and licked at banks and battered bridges.
And all the while, and all-encompassing,
A darker force than flood was in control.
Shapeless, resistless, a dream-engendered thing
That pulsed without a sound to its one goal:
Triumphant tributary under the tide,
Sweeping all else but ocean-crest aside.

"What did the postman leave this morning?"
                                        "Look.
Anonymous, of course. Addressed to me,
But meant for both of us. You know the book?
At least have heard of it. Colette's *Chéri*.
Who does not love Colette? She is so wise!
Nothing concerned with passion can escape her.
Lea the old and Youth before our eyes!"
The little French edition on cheap paper
Turned in the hand as if it were a snake.
I took the book away and kissed the hand.
"My dear, what earthly difference does it make
If some fool sees a parallel? The grand
Lea you are, but never Lea the old."
The lips that kissed my lying lips were cold.

Racing the Smokies storm, we found a cave
That curved beneath the shaggy mountainside.
I piled up stones and built a fire that gave
Comfort while we undressed and shook and dried.
Over the jackpine flames we crouched—like creatures,
I said, left living from the Pleistocene.
But with some reapportionment of features,
O Peking cousin late of Choutoukien?
Agreed. And yet for all our education
That angel-animal who first found fire—
See him in time's spyglass imagination—
Lives in this cave, in us, in our desire.
Be glad for things that link to caveman ways:
Come close, come close, before we lose the blaze.

At Manteo we walked along the beach
Under the spell of gentle sea and sky,
Absorbed in love beyond the urge of speech,
Daring to dream that storms would pass us by.
At night we spread our blanket on the dune
Where tall sea oats etched patterns in the mist,
And whispered to the ocean's sleepy tune
Our litany of tenderness, and kissed.
So safe we were we smiled with disbelief
At village tales of fury from the air
That punished ships and brought the coast to grief,
Until we came one dawn upon the bare
Ribs of a cottage beaten to its side
And heard the serpent hissing of the tide.

When bushy evening held an autumn shape
And streetlights flamed like flowers into bloom,
Absorbed in love, we could not yet escape
A dusty sound outside our curtained room.
To sponge the cricket's dry arithmetic,
We kissed as if we would dispute its sum,
Seeking to reconcile its rhetoric,
We closed our eyes on calendars to come.
Seasons of grief more reticent than song
Would be for us the yield of muted days
When anguished dialogues of right and wrong
Diminished to a brief descending phrase
Murmured against the insect-sounding air:
And each would know what treachery was there.

The program for tonight: Chopin Preludes,
The melancholy ones. Pianist rain
Phrases the soft, rubato platitudes
In cadences that bring their private pain.
We lie in bed lost in the sealing sound
That shuts the world away. We do not sleep
Or talk. We feel the darkness fold around
As the fire flickers and the windows weep.
Along the narrow river of the nerves
Desire, once such a fevered swimmer, floats
In shoals of memory and drifts and curves,
And all night long the rain repeats its notes.
At the first wisp of light we turn and rise
Without a kiss, with lowered, guilty eyes.

In Alachua we saw the coral snake,
Secretive, docile, deadly, half-concealed
Against the sawdust heap beside the lake,
Its carapace of cloisonné revealed.
So like his enemy, the scarlet king,
The walker is imperiled to determine
Which is the sluggish paralyzing thing
And which the unenvenomed foe of vermin.
Remembering my boyhood barefoot lore,
"Red touching yellow, dangerous fellow," I said,
Yet was aware that choice committed more
Than order of colored rings and cobra head.
Only the brave can judge the matter right,
And those who briefly feel the fatal bite.

"Whom have you asked to share our afternoon?"
"Only those youngsters you saw the other day."
"Children adore picnics." "Hand me that spoon.
I said we'd meet them near the woods halfway."
"Their families have farmed these lands forever?"
"And some of them I taught in Sunday school
That summer before—before—now, don't be clever—
Just carry these baskets. I'll take my little stool."
We spread the feast on checkered cloths, and waited,
More and more silent. "Shall we go in?" Meeting
Us on the road, as I anticipated,
They scurried past and would not give us greeting.
"Why should this come as a surprise to you?"
"But not the children, not the children, too!"

Love, do not let the mockers mock our love.
Their voices flat and practical as stone,
Their eyes like ferrets fierce and quick, they shove
And sniff and cannot leave our lives alone.
They foul the flowers that they cannot smell,
And what they cannot comprehend, deride.
Let not these spoilers work their weasel spell
On trails that you and I have walked with pride.
Perceiving now your wounded innocence,
Touching love's fabric marred by their gross stain.
Having no shield against their insolence
Except our private rapture and disdain,
Oh, I would cover your ears, I would cover
Your eyes, cry, Listen only to your lover!

Her words were like a slap across the face.
I winced and prayed somehow you had not heard
Her well-meant greeting in the dining place:
"Is this your mother?" Fury and shame deferred
To cold decorum. Seated, we looked with eyes
Guilty to guard the other. "Shall we go?"
Patrician your response, scorning disguise:
"It does not matter, dear. The world must know."
I might have been your son, who was your lover
And stood accused upon the stony path.
The riddle of love had turns we must discover,
However perilous the Theban wrath:
Jocasta with no children and unwed,
And Oedipus no king, except in bed.

"So now you think you know the awful truth
　What would you have me do? Streak through the streets?
　Limp with a leper's bowl and cry Unclean?
　Offer my legs as posts for every dog?"
"You need not root in garbage like a hog
　To make me sensitive to what you mean.
　The violence with which you foul your feats
　Accuses you of more than being uncouth."
"I beg your pardon for my vulgar speaking
　As I have asked indulgence for my straying."
"Both of us know the answer you are seeking,
　As well as what it is you are betraying."
　Suave thrust, curt parry, so went the ceaseless duel
　Over the grave of love, open and cruel.

Bitter your words and brutal my response
As lightning glared and thunder blared around,
The candles guttering in the silver sconce,
The clock obsessive with its double sound,
The rain battering the lilacs in the yard,
The wind whipping the hemlocks on the hill,
Your eyes like lapis blue, like lapis hard,
My tongue a lance of hate pointed to kill:—
These parallels, so dear to the Romantic,
Are not acceptable, are out of fashion;
Another way, less obvious, less frantic,
Must serve to symbolize the death of passion.
Fashion be damned! This was the way it died,
Raddled with rancor, swollen with sullen pride.

The folly of love like ours was plain to see,
And evident afterwards that we were so:
Searchers for fruit upon that darkest tree
Where no fruit is, where only shadows grow.
The happiness we had was rudely brief,
Enraptured instants gouged from time and taken,
High moments hedged about by hate and grief,
Glimpses of heaven and hell, then heaven forsaken.
Knowing that we were alien, paired with pain,
And that we stumbled in a starved pursuit,
Was it not madness we should seek again,
And thirst the while we sought, the ambiguous fruit?
Yet how could two tormented by long drouth
Refuse the wind rain-heavy from the south?

Like a proud queen in quiet self-exile
Who royally abandons hopes and fears,
Aware no king's decree can win her smile,
No guarded gate admit ambassadors
Petitioning to kiss forgiving hands,
Gently determined not to wound or yield,
She makes a final progress over her lands
And wears her pride in silence like a shield.
Not he. He tongues his rage to rhetoric,
Parses his passion like a boy at school,
Spatters obscenities he prays will stick,
Forgets he is love's prince and plays the fool.
With phrases set to satisfy his art,
Like Hamlet's whore he must unpack his heart.

So it is done, and now we love no more:
Ten ordinary syllables of loss
That will not cause the waves to vex my shore
Or your ancestral pines and oaks to toss.
Love's brief sojourn was no concern of Nature's,
And its demise will neither harm nor halt
Her blind absorption in more primal features
Than lovers' jealousies or fixing fault.
You proved again that you were civilized,
And my aplomb, I think, was not disputed.
We walked within the corridors we prized,
Despite some agony, however muted.
So neither of us swore and neither swooned:
A man can bleed to death without a wound.

I have been false to those who trusted me
And gave their lives and love into my keeping,
Debased their gold with dross and filigree,
And taught them cruel laughter, cruel weeping.
Although I never said that lust was love
Or that the doer was better than his deed,
I worshipped at two shrines, below, above,
Dancing before them both with naked need.
No friend could well defend when others cursed.
Their cold contempt was kind beside my own.
I have betrayed the best, fawned on the worst,
And come at last to find myself alone.
Staring back down the unregenerate years
I see your eyes alight with love and tears.

This body, that has lain so long alone,
Hunts like a dog across the trails of sleep,
Pursuing pungent scent past tree and stone
To fields that shelter, shadow-dark and deep
Beneath the brush and cruel-fingered briar,
Bracken and vine that camouflage the ground,
The elusive quarry that quivers like desire
And now is gone without a trace, a sound.
The hunter crashes through the fragrant ferns
And blunders up the granite-guarded hill
Memory-redolent. He whines and turns
And staggers down to where the lure calls still.
The spreading mist is like a seeping stain.
The hunter wakes and weeps and sleeps again.

A field I meant to buy, a violin,
A book I hoped to read, a book to write,
Countries whose explorations to begin
I had begun alone in bed at night,
Letters to friends perplexed at never hearing,
Visits I promised I would surely make:
All unregretted nothings disappearing,
Gone from my mind, my life, for true love's sake.
And now that love has proved not quite so true,
Not so all-in-all as dreamed for heart and brain,
When we once more are only I and you,
Surely here's time for fiddles, and friends, and Spain.
I brace myself—and then I slump and sigh:
"Alles vorüber . . . es geht . . . alles vorbei."

The auctioneer was clever at his trade
And knew the note to sound, something between
Commercial appeal and snob allure. He played
Deftly upon the crowd and kept a keen
Rivalry running when the dealers bid
For Oriental rugs and Louis XV chairs.
Collectors too he urged to help get rid
Of this small stuff so we could start upstairs.
Three days the sale continued, I was told
By friends who wondered why I did not stay
After the first hour, when I bought an old
French paperback, its pages turning gray,
A golden chain that would not fasten, and
A tiny watch without a minute hand.

FOXTROTS

NEW ENGLAND SIMMER: LOOKING

In Concord Emerson
Looked out and on and on.

Thoreau at Walden Pond
Looked down and then beyond.

While Bronson Alcott sat
And looked around and at,

Margaret Fuller eyed
Her men and looked inside.

Hawthorne, in Brook Farm clover,
Looked back, oblique, and over.

Whittier and Longfellow,
Lowell and Holmes, looked mellow.

And Melville, growling thunder,
Looked ever deeper under.

Alone in Amherst one
Looked lightning at the sun.

NEW ENGLAND SIMMER:
AND LATE AFTERNOON

After such golden days
Came bleaker times for bays.
What energy it cost one
To stay on top in Boston!

Irish fresh from the ships,
With blarney on their lips,
Took over bars and banks:
While transcendental Yanks
Retired more frail and pale
To Harvard and to Yale
(Keeping the spirit steady
With Mary Baker Eddy)
They gathered in the votes
With promissory notes,
And made the better clubs
With money brewed in pubs.
Which proved no drop more dripping
Than money made in shipping
And not a whit less winning
Than money made in spinning.

Latins held up their Cross
To show whose God was Boss,
And Poles and Jews grew hot
To bean the Boston pot.
(Later, a dusky nation
Would bus for education,

Although their integration
Was not, for all, elation.)

Now misters and their madams,
Not Cabot, Eliot, Adams,
Not Edwards and not Mather,
Cultured up a lather,
And people from Out There
Took over Harvard Square.

Not all, meanwhile, was lost,
For Robinson and Frost
Worked barren towns and fields
To harvest golden yields.

Eliot from Abroad
Addressed his muse as God.

Aunt Amy smoked cigars
And lowered metric bars
And fought with Ezra hard:
New England was her yard.

And Edna on her rocks
Opened Pandora's box.

Where Marquand's venomed knowledge
Sufficed in spite of college,
Now peering through old transoms
A protégé of Ransom's,
A younger, stronger Lowell,
Looked back, and black—oh, well.

DIRECTIONS TO THE PAINTER

Delicate green, pale gold, blue,
Effect of fragility,
But with a line to the jaw
And a light in the soft eyes
To indicate ownership.
Informal but expensive
Atmosphere: crushed-velvet fields,
A great house in the distance,
Horses, perhaps, near the fence
On which she rests her soft hand.
Sweater and skirt, string of pearls,
Diaphanous scarf, perhaps.
(Let your clichés do your work.)
Soft clouds, grass and bending trees.
On the fence, honeysuckle:
A few pale yellow blossoms
And stark rendering of vine
To stress the suffocating
Strength of the slender tendrils.
And a plain gold frame, of course.

MEANWHILE, BACK AT THE RANCH
(Movie Suite)

I

"Visible hieroglyphs of the unseen dynamics of human relations."
Certainly one way of putting it, Horace Kallen.
"Writing history in lightning."
Thank you, Woodrow Wilson.
"The motion picture a living organism, the camera its eye."
O.K., Vertov.
"Above all, to make you see."
You said an eyeful, David Wark Griffith.
"The movies have destroyed real time."
Great master Eisenstein! And no pun intended.

Fun to list and to talk about
(Any good book on the subject supplies them),
Points of departure for a certain superiority
That would go on to remark—
Oh, inevitably—
With pyramidal variations of approval,
The contributions of the poet Flaherty,
The symbolism of Dovzhenko and "Un Chien Andalou,"
And the neo-realism of Rossellini,
Not to mention a celebrated cabinet *circa* 1919
And the camera revolution in "The Last Laugh."

And a space all to himself, of course, for Ingmar Bergman.

But these are for courses in the history of the film;
These are not the movies, for most of us.

It is not for these we fly with Goldwyn and his pards
To the temple of the most low Self,
The gilded Bijou or the Dreamex Drive-In or at home
        on television,
Served by those venerable and kindly ticket takers,
Pavlov and Freud.

II

Oh, deep in the freud of everyone
There's a buckskin bronc and a fast six-gun,
There's a Western urge and a saddle surge
And Paramount pills for a pyschic purge.

There's a desert trail and a girl that's true
And a pavlov moon for her and you.
There's a bar-room brawl and a profiled drawl
And Technicolor over all.

There's an Indian hand and a flaming arrow
And a race through the rocks where the pass is narrow
And a last stand of a brave band
Of Mescaleros, Factor-tanned.

Pavlov and Freud.

III

You go to your seat and I'll go to mine.

IV

As, say, the bottom of the sea, say:
Darkly suspended, submerged in sense-murk,
The sanded, quivering-fine antennae
Radiant to the umbilical pulsing:
Anemone, coral, polypean creatures
Opening, say, there in the glaucous rhythm:
The tidal sweep, the visceral agitation,
As, say, the rooted floating of sea-things:
The lovers coming together as lewd as lobsters.
The dispossessed passionately possessing.
The shy, the afraid, proudly and graciously acknowledging
The murmurs of approbation, the hands of homage.
The lonely, the clumsy, now the needed, the clever,
Playing like virtuosi the adoring cluster.
The tentacles of polypean tenderness seeking,
Attaching and sucking under the tided osmosis:
As, say, under the sea, say,
The food of the polypean colony is ingested.

V

How wrong you are, intellectuals, critics,
To mock and despise. Your learning lacks compassion.
After the foreign film is shown on the campus,
You meet to smile at the plot and conjugate the symbols.
In the end you talk only to one another.
You suck upon yourselves in a tight circle.
Straining at gnats, you swallow camels. Wisdom,

Which walks with magnanimity, escapes you.
The stereotypes you deride absorb you.
In the end your own clichés glitter and clutter.
It becomes a bore to talk of the art of the film.

VI

How wise they were, those foxy old makers of movies,
Their wisdom based on greed and a ghetto sadness:
They knew we do not go to the movies escaping;
There is no escape, in or out of the movies,
And the exit lights which rubricate the darkness
Lead only to alleys of night tumescent with terror.
The innocent time when we thought the midnight knocking,
The peremptory summons, was something we read of
           in novels,
Or watched with wet excitement in double-features,
Is over forever. Now we know bitterly better.
We are available now when we are sent for:
The time does not matter, at work, at home, in the movies.

To lay the charge of escape is only delusion.
To talk of facing the truth is self-deception.
It is not to escape, certainly not. Rather,
We cannot endure, they know, the crowded aloneness.
We do not scuttle and settle to lose our being;
We know we are lost already. But we go seeking
The path erased in the woods to the far-off river
That whispered underground, its source undiscovered.
The bed of its promises now smothered in asphalt.

We do not live in this or that or the other
Tower or street or city: we eat or sleep there,
We sit at desks facing ambiguous figures
Or go about receiving or giving service.
But our home is the country of our imagination.
There we are joined once more to what we surrendered,
To selves from which we were sundered. Oh, in the movies
The hills and the sky and the faces are all familiar.
We read the map they spread for us there in the darkness;
There we return to ourselves for a private purpose,
Back to the porch (dark is the porch of our childhood)
Never revealed to the enemy lurking and looking.

In the world outside committees are meeting and voting,
Some one is always watching or sending a memo,
We are never alone, not even now in the toilet,
We are graded and sorted by IBM wardens and nurses:
At last, when our number is up, we are columns of data.

We go to the movies to shape the world to our pleasure,
But we never deceive ourselves that we are escaping.

VII

Consider, at last, the movies as the O.K. corral:
Where the gods of our idolatries, the centaurs,
The men half horse, the horses superhuman,
Are parted for scripted purposes, but never separate:
Deus from the atavistic stallion of cloud:
Paint, Palomino, Champion, Trigger, and Tony:
We spring into the saddle on Little Sorrel,

We stroke Traveler's rosetted flank, we spur
Marengo forward, crying "Tête de l'Armée!"
Back, back to Bucephalus, bridling Pegasus,
Up with Phaeton and the steaming stallions of the sun!
Oh, our Father who never hurls us into the void!
Down from the well-known rock or out of the branches,
Familiar and trusted scene of our yearning vision,
The god leaps, assuming identification,
Bronzed and controlled and austerely controlling.

Oh, in the movies we are all caballeros,
And most of all those who never had horses.
We cross the pastures of our own personalities,
Offering lumps of sugar and mounting and riding.
Oh, in the movies our horses go at a gallop;
They canter over sierras of our innocence.

But we never deceive ourselves that we are escaping.

We know there is no Exit from Box Canyon.

FOIBLES FOR CRITICS

GENEALOGICAL

It may be a virtue, it may be a fault:
From what I can see of the pedigree
One half of them look like their old Uncle Walt
And the other half favor their Aunt Emily.

WHITMAN

Like King Canutes the critics lash his waves:
His laughter thunders in his ocean caves.

EMILY ELIZABETH

Drawn by the radar of her roses
Like helicopter hummingbirds,
Critics hover to taste her phrases.
But suddenly a flash like swords,
Petals up-shield, and tasters gasp:
They sip a flower and eat a wasp.

WILLA CATHER

Writers who get into a lather
Ought to reflect on Willa Cather:
She ruled her mind, she cooled her heart,
And ended up a work of art.

e. e. cummings

Don't be afraid of switchblade knife
And teen-age stance and eyes like stone:
This boy is going steady with life
Like Manna-Zucca's baritone.

FAULKNER

Here's Troy burned and Agamemnon's fits
Served up with black-eyed peas, hog jowl, and grits.

FITZGERALD

Under the aspirin saxophone
And alcoholic trumpet wail
We hear the thorn-embreasted moan
Of Princeton's golden nightingale.

ROBERT FROST

He scythes the landscape with one sure slice
To show us hell beneath New England ice.

THE FUGITIVES

Aristocratic sentimentalists,
They took their stand with bravery and brains.
They waved a tattered flag and shook their fists,
And died of too much iron in their veins.

HEMINGWAY

O youths and maidens, moving hand in hand,
Wind down the labyrinth of love and war.
Come celebrate the ritual of And
That charms our literary Minotaur.

MILLAY

She, more iambic than most girls,
Polished her love affairs like pearls

And, moved by literary fashion,
Strung sweet pentameters of passion.

MARIANNE MOORE

Poetry, seeing Miss Marianne Moore
Come cool and smiling from the zoo,
Nervously straightens her pinafore
And scuffs her ankle with her shoe.

EUDORA WELTY

She is your country cousin come to town.
Before the square piano she sits down
And takes a gospel hymn, and without shock
She counterpoints it à la J. S. Bach.

ANGEL ON THE RIVER

At your hunger and anger and greatness of heart
Even the sternest must soften:
But really, Eugene, in the interest of art,
Must you cry wolf so often?

FALL OF THE HOUSE: EAP

At night,
Alone, I hear
The ivy plunge its roots
Into the stones, thrusting the walls
Apart.

ELINOR WYLIE

Elinor Wylie
Suffered slyly.
She was her own
White jade whetstone.

AUDEN

The Paganini of metaphor whose art
Balances melody of brain and heart
Whose leaps and sweeps and doublestops so please us
We follow this fiddler boy from Freud to Jesus.

WELSH TRIAD

What thing will hurl a man from home?
The curling furling spray of foam.

What thing will lick his starved desire?
The quickened flickering of fire.

What thing will find and bind the lost?
After the foam and the fire: the frost.

ON THE BEACH AT
ANNA MARIA, FLORIDA

Not
> like a myriad snowy mares that race and rear and toss
> their glossy manes, rolling their foam-flecked eyes;

Not
> like the ponderous charge of terrible stallions squealing
> and biting, arching their necks and neighing their
> > stallion cries;

Not
> like the earth-shaking stamping of steeds or the galloping
> crest-curving thundering on-rushing run of horses in
> > any disguise:

But
> fluid and flat where it caught the sun on the curling wave,
> slapping and spattering the rim of the beach and making
> > a roar;

But
> scattering glittering bits of shell and stranding bloated
> jellyfish:—and in no equine metaphor,

But
> entirely confounding rhapsodical fools who have tried to
> stable the sea:—the water, as water comes in, came in
> > to the shore.

PROFILE: CHALK ON BLACKBOARD

1

ROSY

I sat in the departmental meeting
Paying more attention to the chairman's books
Than to his wandering words.
A title caught my attention:
Sing, Rose.
At once my mind was elevated with Dante and Eliot
And of course circular with Miss Stein.
But upon closer inspection
(That required bifocal adjustment)
I saw I had been mistaken,
And came back to the matter under discussion:
Using Prose, it said.
Ah, Monsieur Jourdain!

2

AT A CONFERENCE OF EDUCATORS

The meeting room was very hot.
Outside not a breath was stirring.
Inside a stupor settled.
A mental stickiness affected even the members of the panel.
I was manful with my notes,
But alas, some of them were nonsensical,
And in all honesty I could only half-blame myself.
Suddenly

As we reached the reading readiness of rote songs
In the total integration and adjustment to life situation
Of the core curriculum
Or Something
The wind played a cool cadenza on the Venetian blind
And I put down my ballpoint pen
And listened to the laughter of children.

3

CAMPUS CONCERT

At the Poulenc
Everyone suddenly remembers to look intellectual.
And the professor of art,
Who would rather be damned than acknowledge anything
        before the 1920's,
Bounces alert.

"The moderns have it, they have said it all,"
He declares richly in the lobby during the intermission.

"Except serenity," says the Emerson specialist,
And goes outside where smoking is permitted.

COMMENCEMENT ADDRESS: PLAY LIKE

How much the names of your games and your processes teach us!
It is not patronizing or bland, but sobering, chastening,
To reflect on the view of the world in your playing, O children,
And all the more grim for the grace and the zest of your pleasure.

Consider the concept of IT, the leader, the counter,
Controller of mood and of movement, the lord of direction,
As in Statues, where you must freeze in whatever position
IT flings you, advancing only when IT is not looking.

Or in Redlight, where you run only during the counting,
And the thrill is to match your speed with the skill of the counter,
The numbers deceptively slow, then breathlessly shouted,
And to match your stopping with ITS impetuous whirling.

IT commanding the number and length of the steps to be taken
Before you can touch the tree ahead of the others:
Three Giant Strides or seven Butterfly Flutters,
Only to hear, Go back! You didn't say May I!

And Hide and Go Seek, that game for the longest of evenings,
When the challenge of hearing Ready-or-not-I'm-coming
Is tilted against Home-Free, and the furious racing
Back to the base is like the pounding of ponies.

And the strongest of all, the driving Follow-the-Leader,
Where doing and daring are triggered by fierce emulation,
Pressing and forcing to wilder contortions and climbing
Until IT falters and there is a rush for succession.

The ambiguous games based on the paying of forfeits:
Which hand is it in? and trying to catch IT deceiving;
Or an older, darker perception of IT as the victim,
As in Blind Man's Buff, ITS eyes denied by a kerchief.

And a final game in a circle, with its jocular jingle:
        "Froggy in the Middle and he can't get out:
        Take a little Stick and stir him all about."—
Well done, my dears—now into the world with your playing!

"AN OUNCE OF CIVET"

AGNOSTIC

He wanted to be certain, more or less.
He died and left no forwarding address.

BAROMETER

The young sometimes are cruel to the old
To brace themselves against the coming cold.

FOUR MORE: DALE MURPHY

Despair on the mound:
Shining bird disappearing:
Joy boy at the plate.

MIDNIGHT CALLER

Spring rain at my door,
Tapping out your remorse code,
Who told you her name?

UNDER A BANK OF THRIFT

I slaved and saved, good member of my class:
Now graved, I lie appalled at spendthrift grass.

HOT STUFF

The blessed Angela de Fulgina
Panted to thrust coals into her vagina.
Before she could go off in holy fire
She was forestalled by her confessor friar
Explaining coolly it was not her fate
To offer up her gender as a grate.

WEATHER VANE: GOOSE

Whirled by mountain winds,
His wooden wings spatter rain
Smelling of sea dunes.

SWAN DIVE: GREG LOUGANIS

Thrusting Jupiter
Embraces pliant Leda
Mating air, flesh, wave.

—AND NAGASAKI

Who planted your seed,
O royal chrysanthemum,
In gardens of death?

MAESTRO

So. You took music.
Well. Come back and play for me
When music takes you.

OUT, OUT

The first thing man made
When he teased rubber's secret
Was an eraser.

DO YOU SOLEMNLY SWEAR

Oh, yes, I do believe in Him, DV.
The problem is, does He believe in me?

RARA AVIS: AT A CONGRESS OF COMPOSERS

You see that slender man, the one in grey,
At the edge of the group, who turns his face away?
He never worked with Nadia Boulanger.

DUSTY ANSWER

First whippoorwill calls:
I'll take off my shoes and dance
On arthritic feet.

MOCKINGBIRD

He has learned to quote
Police calls on the highway:
Neon nightingale!

CARDINAL

Are you the red bird
She fed in the snow? Here's seed.
How is your torn wing?

CRITIC

The great whales' singing
Disturbs the calm of the sea.
Hand me my harpoon.

SCOTCH SNAP

Here's evidence of what the years can do:
The Royal Tartan vested on Guess-Who.

GIFT TO THE BRIDE

"If, after all, the pattern is not right
Or if the bowl is duplicated?"
                                    "Quite."
I would to God I could as quickly pack
This passion in my heart and send it back.

BANTY

His crowing cracks the shell of dawn,
Awakes his wives, and eggs them on.
He ruts and struts, his feathers curled,
Cock-sure of all his cock-eyed world.

THE OLD KING

Do you think, my scornful prince,
That only the young ache and groan when love calls?
I tell you old kings too have blue balls.
They wince
And smash their beds and grunt
And rage to snatch your granny's cunt.

LYRIC WITH MISSING STANZA

Prudence enough to seek from love
Only a kiss, a smile.
Wisdom to know that love would go
After its brief, bright while.

So rang the song all summer long,
Prudent and weather-wise.
What thing was this salting their kiss,
Staining their winter skies?

A LAUGHING LADY IS DEAD

She was not good, but she was beautiful,
And life for those she loved was warm and gay.
Her only dread was of the dark, the dull;
And now the dark, the dull will have their way.

PISTOL

Let no cold fingers fumble here
Or thumb my secret hot and near
Until he learns or thinks he learns
Why tears scald and laughter burns.

QUIA MULTUM AMAVIT

May it be said when I am dead
And stand before the gradebook gate,
Enter forgiven the classroom of Heaven.
You sinned for love: Hell is for hate.

VERBUM SAP

I

Respect the pedigree of Word
And tree it to its Sanskrit root,
As you would reconstruct a bird,
Given a breast-bone and a foot.

Trap it in neat linguistic snares
And tag it with the aid of Grimm:
Word *may* escape you unawares,
Wavering off, elusive, dim.

As water into water blends
And is not what it was, nor merely
What it becomes; as Time that ends
Is not Time-Not, yet Time-Not nearly:

So Word, despite austere Semantics
And all the rules to fence and fix,
Crosses Pacifics and Atlantics
And plays us Word-unguessed-at tricks.

Referent needs a referee
As much as any boxers do;
What I would say is clear to me,
Though *Why* not quite so clear to you.

In our own day have we not watched
Gobbledygook receive the blessing

Of Government, a mess so blotched
That Yes means No – or merely Yessing?

What song Sir Thomas' Syrens sang,
What name Achilles took in trouble,
Is no more puzzling than the slang
Of politicians talking double.

Despite your footnotes and your gloss,
Word may not wait to fit your pen.
A dagger thrust becomes a Cross,
A passion cancels Jespersen.

Heightened by moisture in the eye
Or labial impertinence,
His Truth transforms into her Lie,
And Word is stripped of reverence.

A smile can alter Curse to Kiss,
A glance suggest Below the Belt,
Emotional metathesis
Turn what was thought to what is felt.

Printed, Word's neighbors may annex
Or modulate its blunted look;
Spoken, the voice adduces X
For which no answer's in the book.

Worshipped, Word blossoms into Name;
Ignored, it cancers into Fear;
Perverted, is a blot of shame
That rhetoric can only smear.

In the Beginning was the Word.
Or reasonable facsimile.
Translation may be deemed absurd:
Enough at least for holy glee.

The fable of the elephant
And the blind men who knew they knew,
Compared to Word's *dévots*, is scant:
What bloody wars to prove it true!

Take, for example, Liberal:
Now there's a word to start a fight.
Conservative or Radical,
Each side, by Word, knows it is right.

Or Y'All, that in the South is proper
And *never* meant, Sir, singular:
The lance of logic comes a cropper
Trying to pin *that* Is or Are.

And Love, the poets' joy and terror,
Who dares define? Out of the Void,
To make us blush at our crude error,
Comes the dark 'Nein?' of Dr. Freud.

Aristocratic Reticence
Retires before the vulgar What.
No matter: His ambivalence
Avails him naught against the Not.

Word rules the maddest Stock Exchange
That ever cursed the Bourse of Time.

The bids for Reputation range
With little Reason, though much Rhyme.

Southey spewed cantos by the yard
And gushed the waters down Lodore.
He was his Sovereign's favored Bard.
Who did? Who was? The name once more?

Consumptive Keats, dying in blood,
Wrote, as he said, his name in water:
Word washed him clean of Cockney mud
And saved him from the critics' slaughter.

The scrofulous Lexicographer,
Classical Addison and Swift
Anchored their craft against Time's blur.
Yet they broke free, to drown or drift.

Ruskin had purple palsy. Donne
Died twice before he was reborn.
Whether he dies undone again
Is matter for scholars' skill and scorn.

What Shakespeare thought of when he said
In Sonnet 146 'Poor Soul'
Or why he left his Anne that bed
Is known to Shakespeare (and to Stoll).

What *did* St. Paul mean by his Thorn
(II Corinthians, 12:7)?
An epileptic taint? Love-torn?
A phallic thrust? Inquire in Heaven.

When we have smashed the Soviet
Or Russia blows us all to bits,
Whether it be O.K. or Nyet,
Some one must find a Word that fits.

When that Most-Word that spells your You
Defaults, improper substantive,
Adopt another Tried and True
And nurture it, that you may – live?

'Words, Words,' once rang through Elsinore
(To vex the critics ever since).
After unpacking like a whore,
'The rest is silence,' cried the Prince.

AD PARNASSUM

Only amateurs shed tears
When the script calls for weeping.
Remember, it is the job
Of the performer to make
Those in the house feel the score
In music, acting, painting,
Or yes, even basketball.
The soprano who gives her
All for first-act Isolde
May not answer the curtain
For the Liebestod. Bernhardt
Said some cogent things about
Mixing passion and technique.
She was speaking of Phèdre,
But her sense has resonance
For all interpreters. It
Applies to Chopin and Bach,
Shakespeare, Shaw, and Neil Simon.

Sam Johnson would have agreed.
Clear your mind of cant, he said.
Advice especially good
For the Romantic school where
It is often fatally
Easy to substitute high
Motives for lack of talent.
This certainly does not mean
That being sincere is bad,
Artistically speaking

Or writing or anything,
But that too often the weak
Are sincere in sloppy ways.

I remember Lilian Fuchs
Giving a master lesson
At Oswego. A boy played
Something on the viola
Intensely. His eyes were shut,
He swayed, and he breathed in gasps.
Even the hardest-hearted
Would have been impressed by him,
But not by his music. She
Waited for him to finish;
And get his breath; then she said,
Now, my dear, play that again
And make us feel what it says.
And may I suggest you start
Up bow on the doublestops,
Make a slight retard before
You return to the main theme,
And get your D string in tune.
The second time was better.
At least we heard the music,
Not the poor fellow's windpipe.

An exaggerated case,
Of course, but the point is sound.
Those who write windpipe sonnets
Should sit longer on the edge

Of the cold bathtub before
They convince themselves they are
Donne, Wordsworth, or Miss Millay.
Let them forget their feelings
(For the moment) and test their
Metaphors and harmonies.
This is what Horace meant by
Keeping your verses nine years.
Just keeping is not enough:
You must try them up bow, too.

A friend of mine went to play
For Heifetz. She had prepared
The Bach Chaconne, César Franck,
Mendelssohn and Brahms, and such
Great things. What shall I play, sir?
Let me hear some scales, he said,
Major, minor, octaves, thirds,
As slowly as you can, then
As rapidly. Don't vibrate.

(Vibrato is so sincere,
But that is me, not Heifetz.)

We no longer put pebbles
In our mouths, true, and we no
Longer have Demosthenes.

Of course, there are exceptions
To these sensible remarks,
Where the glory of the god

Or the goddess takes over
And the heights are scaled. But they
Don't last long without technique
(And she won't be back next week).

You might begin if you are
Really sincere by looking
Up in a dictionary
All definitions and all
Derivations of your words.

TO BUILD WITH WORDS

To build with words is but to whip the air
And conjure architecture out of rain.
It always was and is and will be vain
To summon nothing up and from nowhere.
Such palaces, however raised with care,
Are only fabrications of the brain,
A curving cave where poets' dreams have lain,
A broken statue on a crumbling stair.
Such work can tumble at an icy wind,
Yet still the magic citadels are made;
And though by every gust their towers are thinned
And in the land of loneliness are laid
Into the dust from which they rose, they still
Must rise again, and so they ever will.

FOXHOLES

BIFOCAL LYRIC

Whatsa matter, Buddy, not amused?
You don't seem overly enthused.
How's this war business look to you?
Hell, it's all in your point of view.
Now what's your metaphor for wars,
The Grim Reaper or Laughing Mars,
The bony finger whetting his scythe,
Or the strutting glory, bloody and blithe?
Take whichever one you wish—
Doc and Fred, they're my dish.

Old Doc War, General P,
A Moose, a Mason, a real M.D.,
Approved by the State—got his degree!
Doc the genial baby-snatcher:
"Yep, it's broke, but we can patch her!"
Picking his nose with his little finger:
"Brother, that last dose ought to bring her!
No cause, Ma'am, none for alarm."
Give 'em a shot in the ass or the arm,
An honest look of red-white-blue,
And a call for, "Boys, it's up to you!"
Sucking his lips and scratching his butt
And shaking with laughter down to his gut:
A sure cure for the clap or the syph—

And if that fails 'em, mind you, if—
There's always Fred to put 'em to bed.

You know Fred, friend of the dead,
Undertaker in gold and lead,
With eyes like worms and voice like snot,
A Treasury smile—and hell, why not?
It won't cost more than we know you've got.
A pine box, a frill of satin,
A flag of honor, maybe some Latin:
"Heard about Johnny—mighty sorry—
But you know, Pro Patria Mori—
Stand back, Ma'am, don't cry on my vest—
Dulce Et Decorum Est."

Doc and Fred, two of the best!

WHITE SANDS

The primal element
Could not contain the fish
That throbbed erect and bent
The earth to his warm wish.

Now thinner symbol, air,
Gaunt leper, cries: Unclean!
Let the last essence, fire,
Consume the bone unseen.

ISLAND, ISLAND

Like water in a movie script
Along this raped beach the sea
Reflects direction of the moon
And douches west delightfully.

In photogenic sequences
The waves caress erotic shores,
Discreetly fanning into foam
Orgastic orchestrated roars.

The moon achieves voyeur effects
Of silverfoil and creamy cloud
And horny palms and sand of which
Chambers of commerce might be proud.

Nothing is here to call to mind
The cybernetic ravishment
That married sea and beach as planned.
Except where spurting Kilroys spent

And marred, but for a little while,
The beddy-by of battle ring.
Except this helmet's rusty slime.
Except this random, condom thing.

A PINCH OF SALT ON CHICKEN LITTLE'S TALE: OR A GOOSE FOR MOTHER NATURE

i

Hey diddle diddle
A rocket a riddle,
Our heroes are off to the moon.
And when they arrive there
How will they survive there?
The same as the rest of us soon.

ii

There was a man in our town
And he was wondrous wise.
He jumped into an airplane
And poisoned all the skies.
And when with all his might and main
He saw what he had done
He jumped into another plane
And flew to the Pentagon.

iii

There was an old Congressman
Voted on the Hill,
And if you are not vigilant
He's voting there still.

iv

Byelo Baby Bunting,
Daddy's gone a-hunting
For an air raid shelter as tight as your skin
To wrap his Baby Bunting in.

v

Jack, be nimble, Jack, be quick.
Keep your mouth shut, Jack, or you'll be sick.

vi

There was an old woman who lived in a shoe,
Had a passel of children but knew what to do:
She counselled her sons to practice precaution
And taught all her daughters the facts of abortion.

vii

Pat a cake, pat a cake, baker's man,
Bake me a cake as fast as you can.
Roll it and spray it with DDT
And put it in the coffin with mummy and me.

viii

Dance to your daddy, my bonny laddy,
Dance to your daddy, my bonny wee.
You shall have a fishy on a silver dishy,
You shall have a fishy full of mercury.

111

ix

Mistress Mary, quite contrary,
How does your garden grow?
With aldrin bells and lindane shells
And chlordane bulbs in a row.

x

Old Mr. Muffit made war for a profit,
Clipping coupons in his vault.
Along came a missile and ground him to gristle
And turned all his sugar to salt.

xi

Bomb shelter hot, bomb shelter cold,
Bomb shelter on the spot nine days old.
Some have it hot, some have it cold,
Some have it quite a lot, nine days old.

xii

Sing a song of science, test tubes of death,
Four and twenty poisons to take away your breath.
And when the sky was opened, the birds began to die,
And afterwards the animals—and when, then, you and I?

xiii

Diddle diddle dumpling, my son John
Went to bed with his gas mask on,
Had a dream in the night and took it off:
And that's when John began to cough.

xiv

A birdie with a yellow bill
Chokes upon my window sill.

xv

Henny-penny, my black hen,
She lays eggs for gentlemen,
Sometimes nine and sometimes ten.
Her rooster's name is Hydrogen.

xvi

Little Boy Blue, come blow your horn;
There's death in the meadow and gas in the corn.
Where is the boy looks after the sheep?
Reading ecology, fast asleep.

xvii

Little Tax Scorner
Sat in Fool's Corner
Eating Congressional pie.
He put in his thumb
And pulled out a bomb
And pieces of people and sky.

xviii

P.O.W. WOW DOW
Whose war art thou?
John Q Public's war
P.O.W. WOW DOW.

xix

Old Mother Hubbard went to her cupboard
To get all her darlings their dinner.
But when she got there, the cupboard was bare:
No water, no air, no nothing no where.
And the old lady cried as they lay down and died,
What a hell of a way to get thinner!

xx

Goosey goosey gander, whither do you wander?
Up stars and down stars and in the moon's chamber.
And there we met an old man Who would not hear our prayers.
We took him by the text book and flung him down the stars.

xxi

Where, oh where, has my little bomb gone?
Where, oh where can it be?
With its fuse cut short and its range cut long,
Oh, bring back my bombie to me.

xxii

Singing cockpits and missiles
Alive, alive-O!

xxiii

No.

NEWSREEL

A newsreel shot of soldiers and horses: New Jersey:
Horses and soldiers being transported by airship.
Patiently those which had carried civilizations
On backs of black and bay and gray and sorrel
Submissively standing and going with gelded acceptance
Into the silver anus, into the belly
After the men so many ages their masters:
One of the soldiers stroking one of the horses,
Soothing and looking into its eyes and saying
Something lost in the mastering ambiguous vibration
That launched the plane aloft with its men and horses
Before the dispassionate eye of the camera shifted
To that whore in the harbor giving us all her gesture.

EXILES

(For the Boat Peoples, 1940's–1980's)

I

Over the mucous flats
Sandpipers stamp eccentric signatures
Erased at once by the obsequious (but expensive)
Waves.
Siccative wind files the saws of the palms,
And tissue-paper gulls,
Pair by querulous pair,
Yelping like beagles spatter the pilings.

With Biblical impartiality
The billion-dollar sun effulges.
This, however and naturally,
Is the sanitary limit of democracy.
Ironies of history are reticent,
But those who sun may read.
The ocean is allotted, the sands are numbered.

From the cabanas of artful unconcealment
Float shouts of triumph
And groans of almost-simulated loss.

His thousands and her ten thousands.

Brisk for all their adagio
And ubiquitous,
The buzzards aloft make parenthetic commentary.
They have seen these things before.

There was a desert and a line of men and beasts.
A pillar of a cloud.

Muted but insistent, trumpet and trombone collide,
The saxophonist picks his teeth, awaiting his cue,
And the ivories smile at the talented fingers.

Heard in that desert the terrible sound of horns.
And the walls falling.

II

Discreetly beyond the costly purfling of the shore,
Only the silence and the waiting.
Ambiguous water slapping harborless hull.
Canaan view from Pisgah wave.
And the anguished cognizance: No miracles permitted.
No parting of the sea.
No walking on the water.

Unto a land that I will shew thee.

Out of a desert led by a vision:
Into may be exile as well as out of.

Truly it was spoken:
A land that floweth with milk and honey,
Purring with petrol and the elaborate informality
More rigid than the Sun King's strictures.

III

Into as well as out of
And the walls falling.

How far away, in eternities of denial,
The little Jew girl big with god.

IV

And always there, always beyond,
The lean sea swelling, the silence and the waiting:
Unto a land:
Outside, of course and naturally,
The carefully stipulated limits
Which subtleties of innuendo have revealed:
Against quotas of rhetoric the prose slap of the tramp steamer.
And the homeless, nameless, faceless statistics of rejection.

They have eaten the bitter herb
They have broken the bread of affliction
They have asked the four sacred questions
And given the four sacred answers

Which do not necessarily guarantee the Four Freedoms.

Now over the beach, louder than the wind rasping the palms,
Than gulls yelping, and horns and cocktail mirth, and
            university laughter
The reply of Cain to a fairly well-authenticated Query.

And the carrion birds wheeling and observing
Brisk for all their adagio.

TV DINNER

You learn a lot from TV.

A recent science special
Through its camera magic
Showed us the world of termites.

One picture troubles my sleep.

Their soldiers have mouths so huge
They cannot feed themselves. They
Must be cared for by the blind
Workers who, helpless, nourish
Their fierce eunuch defenders.

Gorging and guarding, they stood
Within their grim pentagon,
Their weapons magnified and
Highlighted until they were
Monstrous in the living-room.

Docile and never tiring,
The workers fed them, fed them.

All night I hear them eat, eat.

A LITTLE NIGHT MUSIC

In the house, pools of light.
Dancers are diving and swimming.
The voices of lovers are tangled with seaweed hair.
Their laughter is horns blown over the water.

In the garden, pools of darkness.
A wounded man is drowning.

The music is rocks that shatter the waves of the dancing.
At the sounds from the house the man raises his eyes.

Later there will be silence in house and in garden.
There will be silence and blood on the rocks of the music.

FINALE

As if they had been reading the Book of Job,
The sky blackened, the winds whirled and trees crashed,
Buildings collapsed upon themselves. Destruction
Blanketed, blotted, as if Cecil B. DeMille
Had megaphoned the word to his technicians:
This is It. Take and Print. No more rehearsals.
Louder than all the switchboards of Ma Bell,
A voice cried over the roar of the rubble
Like Milton Cross describing Götterdämmerung
For the Saturday afternoon Met broadcast,
With Panizza laying on trombone and timpani.
But what it was calling no one could understand,
Not even the language majors or the Berlitz grads,
Not even the Born Agains with the gift of tongues.
A light more brilliant than the Christmas tree at the
          White House
Descended more slowly than the New Year ball in
          Times Square,
And a form out of Oskar Kokoschka or Jackson Pollock
Loomed larger than any Macy Thanksgiving balloon.
The women screamed, except for some sweating Fem Libbers
Who kept shoving the yelling men aside,
And the men cursed and pushed worse than in the Subway.
Suddenly, as if on a signal from Leonard Bernstein
Batoning the darkest measures of Mass or Kaddish,
Everyone moaned, then fell silent, even
The television people, though their mouths
Stayed open. Terror clotted faces and clothes.

Except for the children, that is. They were enchanted
With the Disney spectacle and stood waiting,
While eating their Tootsie Rolls and blowing their gum,
For Superman to cloak over and fix things up,
Or a shaggy transvestite to appear, barking sure orders,
And making everything all right again.

FOXBANE

RUN FOR YOUR LIVES

In our day
A noise like thunder
Like an earthquake
Like a glacier splitting off and falling into the sea
A sound like the nightmared end of the world
Can be made
By a young man
With thinning hair and thick glasses
And a bad complexion
Crumpling paper or scratching his fingernails across
        a piece of glass
Before an attentive praying mantis.

CYNTHIA GOLIGHTLY

Miss Cynthia Golightly is starving to death.
In the richest nation on the face of the earth,
Whose garbage could feed the rest of the world,
A tough old lady is dying of malnutrition.

Being tough, she is doing it slowly.
Being a lady, she is doing it quietly.

These days Cynthia does not leave her room
Except to go to the drugstore or the grocery.
For a while she was angry, and then frightened, at the prices,
But now she quickly buys what she can and goes home.
And of course to church Sundays and Wednesdays.
Walking tires her more than it used to do,
And she has been warned that the neighborhood,
Where it was always so pleasant for strolling,
Is no longer safe, even for a thin little spinster
In unfashionable clothes, but with a gay spray of flowers
She found at Woolworth's.
                                      Though nowadays
She doesn't like to go in there:
They stand out front and inside they crowd the aisles,
Just standing and laughing, dancing and shoving.
She doesn't mind, except it can be awkward
To have to wait so long to be served.

Mostly she stays in her room with her tatting,
Though there isn't much demand for it now.
Still, it gives her something to send

To the church bazaar and keeps her occupied
(Needlepoint now is too expensive)
While she watches television.

She gives grave attention to the news—
Mr. Reasoner has her confidence,
And Mr. Brinkley is such a gentleman—
Nodding or shaking her head in agreement.
She sits dazed before the game shows—
All that money for those easy words!
She loves the Westerns, especially the Bonanza re-runs.
But it is a commercial which gives her the most pleasure:
She laughs as she sips her nice hot tea
(Which she has learned to take without milk or sugar)
At the pretty pranks of Morris, the Nine-Lives wonder cat,
As he pretends to be finicky and finally condescends
To accept one of the shining cans of the delicious flavors:
Kidney (or Liver) in Creamed Gravy,
Seafood Platter (Fish, Crab, Shrimp),
Scrambled Eggs and Beef, Chopped Platter:

Come along now, Morris! Time for Din-Din!
Oh, the little darling! So clever to do that!
What an appetite! How good it all looks!
How she would like to reach out and pet him
Or have him curl at her ankles under the afghan.

Lately, however, she has been watching TV less and less,
For CP&L have just been granted another increase in
        their rates.
And she no longer reads after she goes to bed

As she loved to do for so many years.
Now she puts on a good old warm sweater, reads her
      evening Psalm,
And turns out the light.

Nighty-night, Miss Cynthia Golightly.

CINQUAINS

* *

Indeed
The bug is crushed   (Reformation)
Under your graceful hand.
But see: the brocade of your gown
Is stained.

* *

Midnight.   (Sapphic Fragment)
The moon has set.
The Pleiades are gone.
The time moves heavily. I lie
Alone.

SUGAR-TITS FOR MEZZO AND MANDOLIN

I: MISS PRIM

An empty heart's a silly thing,
And who should know it better than I?
The memories of love make spring:
An empty heart's a useless thing.
A heart with love in it can sing:
A barren heart can only sigh.
An empty heart's a bitter thing,
And who should know it better than I?

II: MISS TOT

Dirge not because of me and death:
Here in the peace of the western grave,
Released at last, I hold my breath
And smile to know that he can give
What life denied and I had sighed for,
Seeking, seeking, until I died for:
The lips of the earth kissing my face,
The murmur of wind, the dark embrace,
The rhythm of rocks, the music of rain:
Mine now. How small the price of pain.

III: MISS MOON

That night the moon was an orange ball,
And the sky was a scarf of blue,
But I beheld no moon at all,
I filled my eyes with you,
        With you.

Tonight the moon is a silver sphere,
And the sky is a skein of light,
But I can find no loveliness here
And you away tonight,
        Tonight.

IV: MISS IN CROWDED STREET

Alert and freckled as a fawn
Leaving her wood to drink the dawn,
Diana passed. She blazed. There shone
From her wild eyes lights carved in stone,
From which a silver flicker thrown
Hinted hunts and trumpets blown.
Acteon, I stared and dared: but on
She flowed, the vision gone and gone.

ELEGY FOR THE PHAGOMANIACS

Yahoos and Banderlog here
Phagomaniacs upon the land

Swarm
As if fields were bakery counters
Tables of delicatessen   Ess, Ess, Mein Kind
Everything on sale   You want the ninny,
No cash down   honey?

Upon what do these seizers feed
Take and take
Devour time, space, themselves   Was Mann ist

Throw away what they cannot clutch
Or stuff into their munching mouths
(These are phyllophagous days)

Rain down filth
Suckandgorge

And what they do not steal
Stain with excrement
Leave to starve

Factory pricks
Ejaculate their deadly jissom
Into the quivering womb of air   *Leeve moder*

Into the rivers
The lakes

Their toilets seep their turds into the sea

Fish float with white bellies upward
Shorebirds choke in the oil at the edge of the ruptured beach

Across the shaking land in asphalt fury
Roars with red eyes and foul anus
Their god Juggernaut
Rabbits and possums
Lions and wolves
Spread their guts before him
Way paved with bloody fur and matted feathers

His worshipers jerk off in piston idiocy
Don't care if I do die do die do die
Change hands and never lose a stroke
Radios screaming hurl their inheritance
Fucking curves against one another   OK Chicken
To prove which will be
Last man under last tree

Leeve moder, lat me in

TROUBLE IN BAY CITY

(restrained use of sensational material)

Oh, yes, they loved each other
Passionately: In bed and
At certain social functions
They were highly successful.

But the way he listened to
Mozart and knew the Koechel
Numbers; the way he read his
Newspaper backward, lifting
His eyebrows as he picked out
The names of friends; and the way
He qualified his comments
With modest self-disclaimers:

And the way she picked her neck
When she fingered her pearls, and
Was always, always having
To go back into the house
After they had got into
The car, and her dismissal
As if she were amused of
Matters he thought important:

Drove them both mad, really mad.

One morning at the breakfast
Table he killed her with one
Blow of the brass candlestick

From her Aunt Mary, whom he
Had never liked, only to
Discover shortly after
She had already paid him
Her wifely respects in a
Cup of coffee she had poured
In the kitchen and brought him
As he read the newspaper
Softly humming, "Mil e tre."
K Number 527.

HAIKU

In January
    Old men in a thin circle
        Guard each other's eyes.

* *

Fewer, fewer words.
    Longer, longer silences.
        Colder grow the
        nights.

* *

Your 440 eyes
    Ring true to my tuning fork.
        Our music begins.

* *

The hydrangea
    In the garden is like me:
        We bloom on old wood.

* *

After gold flowers,
    Blue days, round hills, rounder clouds,
        Summer fields: this rock.

A LONDON BUS, A BOOK, A DAY, A NIGHT

(In Memoriam: Byron Herbert Reece)

Like some intended masterpiece gone wrong,
London, after the sea and the Irish coast,
Was like a sin against the holy ghost
Of light and love and that great sun-filled tongue
That makes us worshipers of English song—
And no more humble worshiper than I.
The city was swollen and sullen. The rescued sky
Looked smug again. The horror that had been there
Had stained the earlier innocence of air
And left it smudged until it was a lie
Against the harmony of man and rhyme.

All day I had devoured fragments of time
And crossed the centuries, square by shabby square.
Cold and dismayed, I recognized that hate,
Worst heritage of peace, had set its weight
On every face, on every London street.

I caught a bus and fell into a seat
And shivered deep into my overcoat,
Cursing the cold, cursing my aching throat,
But cursing most my still-enchanted heart,
A child that would not learn its alphabet
Of disillusionment without regret,
But puzzled out a soft romantic part
When all the world had turned, Medusa-eyed,
To joyless stone.
                        A rustling made me start:

The girl who huddled frowning at my side
Was reading as she rode. The blinded look
She lifted and then lowered to her book
Was welcome-home to me, who had so often
Watched eyes like these first blaze, then blur, then soften.

We might have been divided by a wall:
She did not know that I was there at all.

I knew the book she read; had known the man
Whose blood and pain had gone into the tale
That sealed her now. Along a flashing trail
Imagination beckoned, and I ran.

Elk Mountain brooded over Beaverdam
On that hot day those years ago. Clouds swam,
And breezes curled the edge of afternoon.
Out of the Georgia hills a poet had come
To spend the day with friends who were my friends.

Our generous host had brought us to his farm,
A place of pine and rhododendron charm.
However shy a man, his shyness ends
Where mutual respect extends its boon;
And though our talk was small, it was the kind
To satisfy good sense yet not alarm
The brooding watchers of the poet's mind.

He had been very ill, and even now
A kind of courteous endurance etched
His mouth and eyes. We talked while our host fetched

Our bottles from the spring; we mused on how
The artist's life was nourished on his pain,
The servant-master artery that stretched
Its length from fevered sense to cautious brain.
Although we laughed to lighten solemn speech,
There was a gravity that lent its grace
To the commitment of our thought. The place
Would be remembered in the life of each.

Dead friend, my words have come, like yours, to nought.
Your Georgia hills, my Carolina hills
Preserve their granite mystery that chills,
Their curving innocence that lures and lies,
Makes impotent the thinker, mars the thought.
Nous n'irons plus au bois. Coldness comes down,
Indifference sucks the sun, pollutes our skies,
And darkens us as black as London town.
Yet on that bus beside that reading girl,
In spite of fog that sent its fingers stealing
To write on windows with a warning swirl,
I felt again, and blessed us both for feeling,
The radiance reflected from that light
That warmed me through the bitter, gathering night.

> The book was *Better a Dinner of Herbs* by
> Byron Herbert Reece.

THE UNPOSSESSED

Lovely and fleet and haunting forever,
Where are you hiding whom we must follow?
The aspens are shaken and thin by the river,
Summer's forgotten the flight of the swallow,

The river runs with a single voice,
The skies are still, and nothing flying.
Winter comes on with a mournful noise,
And all night long the wind is crying.

Blind us with snowflakes, cover us deep!
All that we have is the wind in our hair.
Ice in our hearts, let us settle to sleep,
Lost in our dream of finding you fair.

FOXFIRE

VIRGILIAN VARIATIONS:
SONNETS ON CELLOPHANE

"Omnia Vincit Amor"

1

Foolish the man who brags of foxing Love
And swaggers and smirks and preens his idiot lies.
Suddenly arrows edged with fire—whereof
Love's poison is—prick him and hush his cries.
The bowman has a bag of tricks and uses
Them all. The wildest or the wariest,
Driven to lewd or labyrinthine ruses,
Only alerts the laughing tracker's zest.
You cannot hope to fool the pressing foe:
Redoubling on your stealthy steps with speed
Signals your flight, and tantalizing-slow
He follows after you with grace and greed.
Love hunts all men: no matter what the shapes
Or stratagems they dream, not one escapes.

2

As a sure surgeon challenging a cancer
(His mind released of all except the act
Of violence to propagate the answer
The cringed flesh cries for, medicine the fact
Of terror, cull the ulcer's angry core,
And check the fester at the fester's center)
Fingers his scalpel, lifts his hand once more,
And touches the spot the knowing steel must enter:
So too in love, that has no convalescence,

The antiseptic mind, removed from passion,
Warrants and searches, noting the recrudescence
Of epidemic symptoms in clinic fashion,
Dresses the wound, and reads the fever chart
That marks the fluctuation of the heart.

3

This virile beast, angelic in repose,
Purrs and permits himself to be adored,
Allows his flaming eyes to glaze and close
While worshipers caress their couchant lord.
Maidens weave garlands for his regal mane,
Androgynes plait his supple tufted tail,
Priestesses chant, and priests add their refrain
And serve his supper from a jeweled grail.
Yet this suave animal is dangerous:
He has been known to leap without a sound,
Spreading his golden theogonic thews
To savage his celebrants upon the ground
And leave them mangled in their ravished pride
When that dread appetite is satisfied.

4

Falling in love again at sixty-eight!
Surely a cause for comment here or there:
Lacking in teeth, but lacking not in weight,
Tri-focaled eyes, and silver-hackled hair.
"Come now, look at yourself ! A word of warning!
Your almanac has lost its sense of season.
Love's song is programmed for the golden morning.
Time gives no encores."

Thus with me wrestled reason,
That tried to chide and guide from folly's brink
The sweet, ambiguous muscle of emotion.
"But love is Sanforized and will not shrink."—
I heard my heart and leaped into the ocean.
Sages and saints, condemn me as you will:
Campaspe saddles Aristotle still.

5

She lifts her fragile hand: at once he bends
To grant her wish deliciously expressed.
Suspicion spreads among his famous friends
That he has lost his wits, who was their best.
Committees wait, are cancelled, wait again,
Business suspends, while she, grand-daughter's age,
Makes up her mind—gold or platinum chain?—
And ministries implode from stifled rage.
He who was Genghis Khan, whose frown or nod
Convulsed the bourse and turned investors pale,
Whose Up or Down was like the word from God,
Now barks when bade, rolls over, chases his tail,
Brings her bright stones, and fetches fancy sticks:
Who says you cannot teach old dogs new tricks?

6

He types the words, "I am in love with you":
At once the pet pentameters appear,
Trailing their syllables of gold or blue,
Wailing their platitudes cloudy or clear,
Iambic order trivial or true,
According to the mood, the time of year,

145

The latest style of mask—*que voulez-vous?*—
Apollo's shining smile, Silenus' leer.
(Castrated now by the whiplashing rhyme,
The stammered agonies, the sweat, the rage
That churned the heart and turned the blood to slime.)
How wet they look upon the thirsty page!
They lick their faces as their tails beat time
And take their places in the sonnet cage.

7

The fundamental fact of life is death.
It is for death that we are born, are thrust,
Wailing or willing, to run before the wrath
Of time's pursuing, unforgiving ghost.
We stagger our day beneath the dusty weight
Of others whose faces we have never seen;
Their guilty hands set snares to foul our feet;
Our voices join their voices, groan on groan.
Yet though we know the end of life is merde
And that we lie to legendize escape,
One ray illuminates the cave, one word
Pronounces, out of bleakness, blackness, hope.
We bear a cruel burden into the grave:
But to be borne because of one word: Love.

"THEY FLEE FROM ME,
THAT SOMETIME DID ME SEEK"

One day, more likely one night,
They will not come when I summon them.

Already they stay longer and longer in their dark holes.
I hear them rustling and whispering against one another,
Making wispy challenges and chitterings the straining mind
Cannot quite take hold of.
Oh, sometimes now when I send for one,
Another, something like in coat or coloring
Yet again showing no kinship,
Will stalk confidently forth,
Shine at me a baffled moment,
Then falter and stumble back in,
Nipping and nudging those ranging around him
Or blocking the path, churlishly growling.

Once so eager, gentle, tame, and meek,
Happily coming unsought for,
Leaping in lovely precision:

Now only my humbled patience not yet entirely desperate
Brings them out as I need them,
And in the light their coats are sadly diminished,
Their ribs show, their eyes no longer shine, they make
        pitiful whimperings.

One day, or worse one night,
They will not come when I send for them.
They will crouch in the grey corridors,
Rustling and whispering closing to silence in the darkness.

And then the time when I will not seek or send.

INTERVIEW DELETED FROM
THE LIFE AND LETTERS

Now you have scaled the highest peak
What have you learned you did not know?
The air is easier below.
The eagle has a cruel beak.

The vulture has a cruel eye
Floating above a man alone.
A man can learn to sleep on stone.
There is no limit to the sky.

Were you not fearful of the rocks?
They taught me lessons of the lynx
(They are more sudden than one thinks)
As well as wisdom of the fox.

What did you think of as you went?
Whether or not the final cliff
Would keep me from the top, and if
I reached it, what the climbing meant.

What did it mean, what you attained?
I have forgotten how I felt.
I rather think I must have knelt
To rest my body, which was strained.

Did you not speak? Did you not pray?
To whom? For what? In that chill air
I had no thought or breath to spare.
I may have done so on the way.

What drove you harder, gold or fame?
Neither. I cannot now recall
Why I went on. Except that all
Down there was ready with its blame.

Then did it meet your expectation?
Only the going up was good.
After the climb I understood
The emptiness of isolation.

What did you see, looking around?
Nothing I care to speak of here.
Some bones, a broken tree, a sheer
Descent, holes in the frozen ground.

Were there no vistas to inspire?
Oh, there were ranges stretching out
That offered challenges, no doubt,
But none of them was any higher.

Did you remember those who cared
And called encouragement to you?
I spoke their names. I never knew
The path they took or how they fared.

What happened to your faithful friends?
I cannot tell. A storm came up.
The path grew dark. I could not stop.
Or turn. I needed both my hands.

What message would you send to them?
If any ask, say I have none.
What will you do, now you are done?
Wait for the final fall to come.

Would you advise others to try?
Advice is vain. Each man will be
Driven by what he needs to see.
No one can build another's sky.

Would you deprive him then of hope?
Let him address whatever ghost
Will lift him up, but let him most
Depend upon his axe and rope.

EVENING SONG AT BETHANY

Death came mincing in at the door.
Death knows well how to play the whore.
Her hands and arms were thin and white.
Her curving hips bargained delight.

Death came smiling and called me there.
I did not taste the milky breath.
I did not touch the snaky hair.
"Only for Life!" I answered Death.

SIDNEY LANIER AT RICHMOND HILL

Fading to dun and fawn and freckled dark,
Evening achieves the sky. A while ago
Warm rose and gold and that especial blue
I have not seen elsewhere in God's blue world
Were musical outside our tent, and then
The birds matched music with the passing day:
Redbird and catbird and that mockingbird
You said had surely followed us from Macon—
And one small song we could not nominate—
We searched the trees, but found only the song.
"A phrase a flautist would take pride in shaping—"
Remember?—and you, distressed to think me sad
Because I play no more—dear heart, I know—
Took up my hand and kissed it tenderly.

But Mary, love, believe, I am not sad.
That theme had its development, resolved,
Blending with all-surrounding harmony
We hear about us if our ears, our hearts,
Are worthy of God's hearing. Baltimore,
The orchestra, the sense of reverence
I felt in being dedicated so:
All had their contrapuntal place. We rest—
And what in music's life is lovelier
And more life-giving to the speaking phrase
Than silence continuing to sing? We rest
Before we make once more our entrance. So,
It is enough. I am not grieved because
I can no longer spiral silver stars.

Once in the War I made a resolution—
It came from God, and He has helped me keep it:
As He had given me the flute, to make
My little music glorify His name—
And what besides His glory can avail
Our hearts, our lives, the music of love itself?
(That bird again! It sings, then, after dark.)—
All in His time I would lay down the flute,
As I had held it up, all in His time.
And so with song. And so with mortal life.
I learned to pray to understand His will,
But if no understanding came with prayer,
Nevertheless His will. War taught me this
(The lesson was not lightly memorized)
And you, my love, confirmed the learning. Only,
It has not taught me yet to spell good-bye.
But that will come: all comes in its own time.
And so I am not sad, however ill,
However poor, for I am richer here
And happier with you than golden kings.

Simply, another phrase unfolds, and we
Must hear the harmony and take our parts.
Life's symphony is fugal, as in our dreams.
And if I leave you anything, my love,
I leave you this upon the edge of death:
There is no power beyond the power of dreams.
That music rises from a secret place,
Its channel never charted, its vague depths
Unknown, mysteriously swirling—where?
Upon the tide of this far stream there floats

A sterner beauty, such as dared no man
Ever to ponder in the common day.
Our dreams are things to puzzle and bewitch,
To make us frowning gapers into the sun,
Wizarding us with moonlit sorceries
Of all the interwoven web of night,
Lucent and sirenous and singing more,
Although we cannot fathom them as yet,
Than anything our tortured minds conceive.
Dear heart, let us be worthy of our dreams.

We have been troubled and afraid and sad.
Our eyes have ached for what they could not see,
And in our hearts there was an emptiness.
We questioned, we wept, we prayed, and there was pain.
But tented here upon this hill of love,
Grateful to kinsmen and to countrymen,
When Death comes in his opal majesty,
Let me go out to meet him with a cry
Of joy, and so exalt the power of dreams.
Ambiguous and blind between two walls
Our lives are limited. No desperate inch
May they be strained or overstretched. They stand,
Pitiless barriers we can never pass,
Except in dreams, and in that purest dream
That is God's secret and the end of dreaming.

Dear love, forgive this fevered rhapsody.
Your hand. Ah, it is good to hold your hand,
Even upon the edge—no more—no tears.
Tomorrow, then, we shall go down the hill

And track the Pacolet, where it foams and turns
And sings itself among its giant rocks.
We shall have fellowship again with grass
Where we can hear the whistle of hidden quail,
A last flute-song far in the darkening grain.
Let us go down to evening land, my love,
Where slithering winds at twilight over the corn
Are sweet and smooth, all-care-dispelling sounds.
We shall sustain our dreaming in that place
Where mountains lift their seven-fold Amen
After the benediction of the sun.

The Georgia poet camped at Richmond Hill, on the west bank of the French Broad River near Asheville, shortly before his death near Tryon in 1881.

THE MUSIC OF THE SPIRIT

The music of the spirit, never measured,
More all-euphonious than any sound,
More grandly modulated and more round
Than any tone that earthly ears have treasured,
Flows down unceasing from an astral source.
How fortunate and god-like is the man
Who has the happy accident to scan
Its starry page and hear its high discourse.
The music of the mind is struck from chords
That bear the burden of a mighty theme,
Concinnity of chaos in a dream
That wakes to soar with never-weary winging.
Half-heard, uncertain of its own rewards,
The music of the heart is broken singing.

MIDNIGHT, DECEMBER 31, 1975

The year went out in wind and rain
As if the admiral in charge
Were making fleet intentions plain
By semaphoring bold and large.

Since first galactic lightning crashed
And time awoke and stood erect,
Signals austere from stars have flashed
To let earth know what to expect.

For what dark warning may be worth,
Tonight there seemed enough ahead
To cause a friend of light on earth
More than a passing thought of dread.

I walked across my target hill,
Squinting into the New Year night:
Powers above, below, must kill
To win this war of dark and light.

Whatever it had planned for oaks
Within the branches' tortured space,
Despite the wildness of its strokes
The storm was welcome to my face.

I questioned neither cold nor wet,
Having some weather of my own
I hoped they'd help me to forget,
However hard on flesh and bone.

Beneath the storm-tormented trees
I said a prayer, who seldom pray,
Careful to add a cautious Please
To celebrate the Special Day:

Who or whatever rules on form
Tonight in our two-hundredth year,
Let it come straight after the storm,
Let it wash clean, let it blow clear.

If not, may year-end wet and cold
Excite in us when night is gone
Postures we find it wise to hold
Before the final, awful dawn.

Whether or not my brief petition
Rose higher than the white oaks' crest,
Cold comfort granted wry permission
To end the New Year night in rest.

SINGING TREE

This tree made music for your fathers' ears.
A dulcimer for spring to tune and strum,
A summer fiddle to bow away their fears,
Autumn's gold horn, and winter's shadow-drum.

Now in your day the music, though diminished,
Spreads still, over the years of sun and storm,
Its leafy ceremony never finished,
Those airs your fathers cherished, chill or warm.

So in the time when you will not be hearing,
Yourself one note in fuller harmony,
May others of your kind come to this clearing
And hear, as you have heard, your fathers' tree:

Old melodies against the sunset bars,
Rooted in rock and whispering to stars.

A DANCING FOX

was typeset in 12 pt. Deepdene, a face designed by
Frederic W. Goudy. Poetry titles are in 14 pt.
Deepdene. The metal type was produced on a
Monotype casting system at Out of Sorts
Letter Foundry, Mamaroneck, NY.
Paper stock is 80 lb. Mohawk
Vellum. A Dancing Fox was
designed at Birch Brook Press,
Otisville, NY.

FRANCIS PLEDGER HULME

grew up in Asheville, North Carolina, the Smoky Mountain region he celebrated in his first two books of poetry, Come Up The Valley *(Rutgers University Press)* and Mountain Measure *(Appalachian Consortium Press).* "The real, unmistakable magic" *the Library Journal said of* Come Up The Valley, *which the Saturday Review praised for its* "lively ballads" *and* "fine-spun lyrics and sonnets." *Mountain Measure, winner of the Thomas Wolfe Literary Award and the Arnold Young Cup from the N.C. Poetry Council, was impressive for the vigor of its ballads and its melodic appeal.*

Born in Hawthorn, Florida in 1909, Hulme received his A.B. from the University of North Carolina, Chapel Hill, his M.A. and Ph.D. from Emory and the University of Minnesota. He retired as Professor Emeritus from the State University of New York at Oswego, where he founded the program of Graduate Studies in English. A Phi Beta Kappa, Fulbright Professor at New Asia College, Hong Kong, visiting Professor of English Literature at the University of York, England, he taught at Warren Wilson College after his retirement. Hulme was an accomplished violinist who played with such symphony orchestras as Minneapolis, Cincinnati, Atlanta, and North Carolina. Poet, musician, critic— known to generations of readers and students as fph—Frank Hulme was loved for his generosity, respected for his erudition, envied for his unique wit, and admired for the lasting perception of his art, so abundantly evident in A Dancing Fox. *He died in 1986.*